Divine Guidance
Daily Angel Tarot Reading
A daily guide to finding clarity and insight

Amanda M Clarke

KORU (Maori:NZ)
A symbol of spiritual growth and spiritual connection.

Second Edition

The book features a complete set of tarot, each with its AI Van Gogh generated images that incorporate traditional symbolism and modern interpretations and mantras

Tarot deck re-shuffled 7 times!

This book includes all 78 Arcanas of Tarot, the Major Arcana and the Minor Arcana. In this second edition of "Daily Angel Tarot Reading," the order of the cards is determined by clearing my cards and shuffling the deck seven times to produce the random order.

Copyright © 2023 by Koru Lifestylist

All rights reserved. All content, materials, and intellectual property in this book or any other platform owned by Koru Lifestylist are protected by copyright laws. This includes text, images, graphics, videos, audio, software, and any other form of content that may be produced by Koru Lifestylist.

No part of this content may be reproduced, distributed, or transmitted in any form or by any means without the prior written permission of Koru Lifestylist. This means that you cannot copy, reproduce, or use any of the content in this book for commercial or personal purposes without the express written consent of Koru Lifestylist.

Unauthorized use of any copyrighted material owned by Koru Lifestylist may result in legal action being taken against you. Koru Lifestylist reserves the right to pursue all available legal remedies against any individual or entity found to be infringing on its copyright.

In summary, Koru Lifestylist © 2023 holds exclusive rights to all the content produced by it, and any unauthorized use of such content will result in legal action.

The Answers You Seek

Are Within

How to use this book

You are a spiritual being and you have many guardian angels with you, whispering loving and accurate words of guidance to you. Always with you, guiding you to a happy, healthy, helpful, and loving way of being. They whisper to you in many codes, voices, and symbols which you do not always know to interpret or understand.

Angel Tarot is a powerfully effective and safe healing practice that will help you to release fears and emotional blocks, find purpose in your life and help answer your deepest questions. The angels, archangels, spirit guides or whomever your preferred deity is surrounding you right now, and are governed by the universal Law of Free Will, which states that they can't intervene in your life unless you permit them.

Many people like to use Tarot Cards and Tarot Guide Books to learn about tarot and to practice doing personal readings for themselves, I designed Daily Angel Tarot Reading as a book for its' simplicity, quickness and ease of use. You can take it with you anywhere and do a quick reading whenever you are stuck in thought, need to make a decision or are unsure of anything throughout your day. With this book and help from the angels, you will release your fears, cleanse and calm your mind, heal and help you enjoy physical strength and vitality, so that you can move through your day with courage and a clear conscious mind.

Here are the steps you need to do to give yourself (or others) an Angel Tarot Reading.

STEP ONE: CLEAR YOUR BOOKS ENERGY

Since your book is a sensitive instrument and has been through many hands to reach you, you will need to clear it of any energy it may have absorbed. Steps One and Two only need to be completed every so often when the energies of the book become clogged.

It is a good idea to ground yourself first before clearing the book. Do this by sitting on a standard kitchen chair, with your feet comfortably flat on the floor. You can do this with shoes on, but it is better in bare feet. Better still, stand barefoot on the ground in the open, this will ensure all energies will be fully grounded out into the nothingness of the earth.

Hold the book in the palm of your non-dominant hand as this is the hand that receives energy.

Form a fist with your other hand and knock on the book once with your fist sending all energies from the book to the ground and into nothingness.

This clears out the old energy and the book is now blank and is ready to be imbued with your energy.

STEP TWO: CONSECRATE THE BOOK

Flip through the pages of the book ensuring you touch every page with your thumb, fingers or hand. This will start infusing it with your energy.

Hold the book in your dominant hand up to your heart and think about the prayers or intentions you would like to infuse the book with. For example, you may say to yourself in your minds-eye or out aloud:-

"I ask that all of my readings with this book be accurate and specific, and bring blessings to everyone involved. Please help me stay centred in my higher self so that I may hear, see, feel, and know the messages that wish to come through these readings"

Ask the angels, archangels, spirit guides, or whatever deity you are comfortable with, for whatever help you would like during your readings, such as confidence, clarity, compassion, and so forth. Your book will now carry your vibration and intentions.

You may wish to keep your book wrapped in a silk scarf or special bag after this step to keep other people's energies from transferring to your pages.

STEP THREE A: INVOKE INNER CONSCIOUS LEVEL 1 (practice version)

In this step, I will take you through a mindful meditation so you can learn to reach your 'Inner Conscious Level' of mind. At this level of mind, your mind will clear and centre and your focus on your questions and intent become steel. Practising this step at least 3 times a day for a week you will be able to invoke your 'Inner Conscious Level' within seconds. Eventually closing your eyes and touching the tips of your thumb, index and middle fingers will bring your mind directly to the 'Inner Conscious Level'. Let's practice:-

- Find a quiet spot where you can sit comfortably, feet grounded. You may even lie in your bed as in this meditative state you remain conscious.
- Draw in a long deep breath and as you exhale long and slow, close your eyes.

- Draw in another long deep breath, this time as you exhale slowly, visualise the number 3 and in your mind say 'Three' 3 times.
- Stay at this level 3. In your mind's eye, sense a warm slow flow of syrup being poured on the crown of your head. As this warm flow touches each part of your body, feel a deep sense of relaxation come over you. Your scalp, your forehead, your face, your throat, your shoulders, your chest (skin & inside organs), your abdomen, your spine, your arms, wrists, hands, and fingertips. A warm sensation, tingling, circulation. Relax. Your lower back, your hips, your thighs, your knees, your calves and shins, ankles, feet, souls, and toes. A warm sensation, a tingling, circulation. Relax.
- Draw in another long deep breath, this time as you exhale slowly, visualise the number 2 and in your mind say 'Two' 3 times.
- Visualise in your mind, as if you are projecting onto a screen out in front of you, like you a watching a movie at a theatre ... the theatre of your mind. Visualise the most peaceful, serene, quiet place that you know. See yourself there ... lying on a beach watching the water lap to the shore, maybe walking through a grassy forest or floating on the water. Whatever the scene is for you make sure to project all the colours, sounds and feelings onto the screen of your mind. Look out to the distance. At this level of mind, any outside sound that you may hear will take you deeper and deeper into relaxation. You won't hear what is being said or care about where the noise came from. You will just sink deeper and deeper into a very relaxed way of being. Keep feeling the visualization of your peaceful, serene, quiet place. Your secret hideaway. Relax.

- Draw in another long deep breath, this time as you exhale very slowly, visualise the number 1 and in your mind say 'One' 3 times.
- Now you are at level 3. Inner conscious mind. But, let's take you deeper. Count in your mind slowly from 10 down to 1. With each count you will fall deeper and deeper into your inner conscious mind... 10, 9, 8 deeper. Relax. 7, 6 go deeper and deeper. 5, 4, 3 you are going deeper still. 2 and 1. You are now deep within your inner conscious mind. Stay here for a moment.
- Whatever hand you are most comfortable with, or you can do both hands. Gently touch the tips of your thumb, index and middle fingers. Lightly at the tips. Sit with this feeling.
- Focus your attention on the lightness of this touch, the tingling as the nerves reverberate around the tips of the fingers. Circulation creates a warm feeling. Feel your whole body disappear into nothingness. Blank. Floating in the darkness. Deeper and deeper you are relaxing. Your mind is still awake, alive but all you can feel is nothingness and the tingling at the tips of your fingers. From here on in and with as much as 3 times a day practice on this 3 tips technique, you will eventually go to inner conscious mind level 1 instantly. To reach inner conscious level 1, you will just touch the tips of your thumb, index and middle fingers and it will bring you to this level of the relaxed conscious mind.
- Count from 1 to 5 and ease back into the conscious mind. 1, 2 easing up, feeling an awakening. 3 when you awaken you will feel better than you did before. You will feel wonderful, and alive. 4 you can blink your eyes with your eyes still shut, 5. Open your eyes. You feel much better than you did before, you are fully conscious almost like you have just experienced the best power-nap

STEP THREE B: INVOKE INNER CONSCIOUS LEVEL 1

If you have been practising the above Step Three A, you should now be apt in invoking your inner conscious level 1 almost instantly.

Start by finding a quiet place where you can sit or lie down comfortably without being disturbed.
Close your eyes and touch the tips of your thumb, index and middle fingers and take a long slow deep inhale. Then exhale long and slow. Release and relax. You are now in your inner conscious level 1.

STEP FOUR: ASK A QUESTION/CHOOSE A PAGE

Think of a question you would like the answer to in your inner conscious level 1. The angels and archangels will hear your thoughts. In your mind think of your question as you flip through the book. You may flip backward and forward until ... you feel the sense to stop. You may even hear in your thoughts "Stop". The law of attraction will always ensure the page you land on is correctly chosen for you, so if you have a feeling of stopping too soon or too late, 'delete' that thought and know that the page you are on is the correct page for you, your question or your daily read.

Hold your hand on the book/page to keep the page open. Count 1, 2, 3, 4, 5, and open your eyes. You will feel a sense of calm.

STEP FIVE: READ THE GUIDANCE, INTERPRETATION AND MANTRA

Take a deep breath in and read the page your hand rests on. You will learn about the tarot that has been chosen, an interpretation and a mantra.

During reading the page, pay close attention to your thoughts and feelings. All senses play a part in your reading. You can repeat the mantra as many times as you would like.

JOURNAL PAGES

Near the back of the book, you will find journalling pages. Write your thoughts, and feelings or scribble doodles at will. Opening a reading page on a blank page can mean that you already know the answer within yourself. By doodling or writing at will, you will feel and/or inscribe the message your guardian angels wish you to know.... enjoy this book!

The Answers You Seek

Are Within

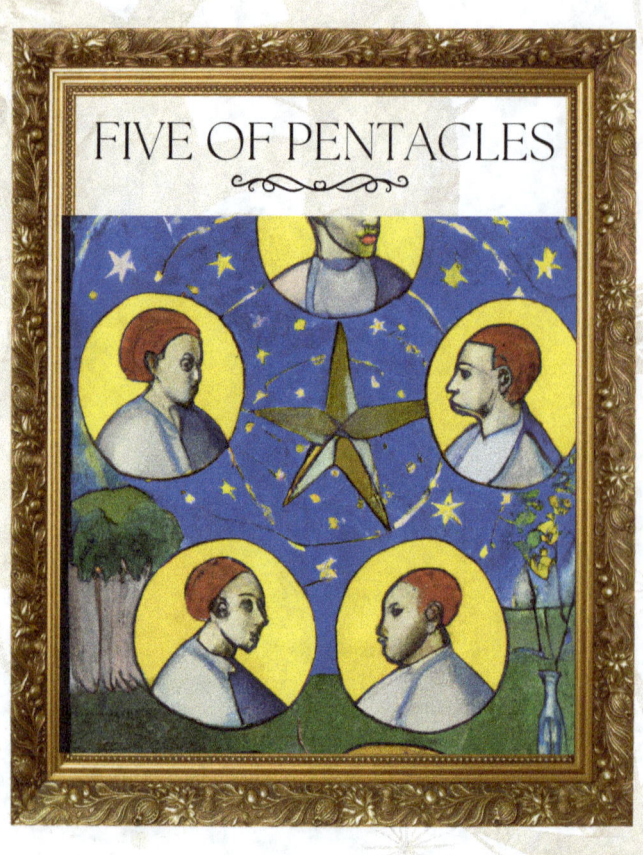

The card the guides have chosen for you is...

The Five of Pentacles is a tarot that typically represents hardship and financial struggles. It can also symbolize a lack of resources, whether they be financial or emotional, and a sense of being left out in the cold. The imagery often depicts two people, usually dressed in rags, huddled outside a church or other place of worship. This can suggest that the person for whom reveals the Five of Pentacles may be going through a difficult time and feeling a sense of hopelessness or despair. The Five of Pentacles can also indicate a need to seek help from others or from a higher power. Additionally, it can also indicate that despite the hardships, one should not give up hope and they'll find a way to overcome the difficult situation. Overall, the Five of Pentacles is struggle, but also one of endurance and the possibility of eventual betterment.

Interpretation and Mantra...

You are encountering financial setbacks, hardship, and a sense of seclusion and solitude. Assistance is within reach, but you are too fixated on your financial issues to perceive it.

Mantra: "I am strong and resilient in the face of hardship. I trust that abundance and security will come to me."

The card the guides have chosen for you is...

Death represents transformation and change. It is not a literal death, but rather a symbol of the end of one phase of life and the beginning of another. It can indicate that a major change or transformation is on the horizon and it is time to let go of the old and embrace the new. The figure is often depicted as a skeleton or grim reaper, representing the end of something, but also the promise of new beginnings. Death can indicate the end of a relationship, a job, or an old way of thinking. It can also indicate the need to confront and overcome fears and insecurities.

In a positive light, Death can represent the end of a difficult period and a new beginning filled with possibilities. It can also indicate personal growth, self-discovery and the ability to rise above difficult situations. In a negative light, it can represent resistance to change, fear of the unknown and a refusal to let go of the past. It can also indicate a tendency to hold on to unhealthy patterns or relationships. Overall, Death represents the natural cycle of life and the need to let go of the past in order to move forward.

Interpretation and Mantra...

You are undergoing a profound shift and metamorphosis. Certain aspects of your life are deteriorating and disintegrating, paving the way for fresh opportunities to surface.

Mantra: "I welcome change into my life. I embrace life".

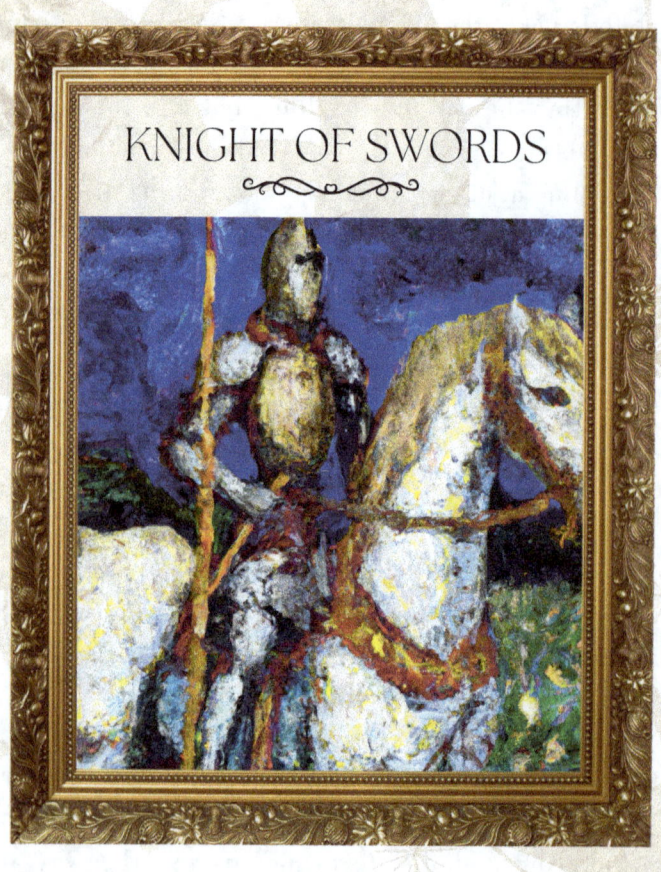

The card the guides have chosen for you is...

The Knight of Swords tarot represents action, communication, and decision-making. He is often depicted on a horse, symbolizing his swift and bold actions. The Knight of Swords is known for his quick thinking and decisive nature, and often represents a time of rapid change and movement. This can indicate a need for clear and concise communication, as well as a willingness to take bold and decisive actions. The Knight of Swords can also represent a desire for independence and the pursuit of one's goals, and can suggest a time of exploring new ideas and perspectives. However, this card can also indicate impulsiveness and a lack of caution, leading to hasty decisions and potential mistakes. The Knight of Swords tarot is a powerful symbol of action, communication, and decisive action.

Interpretation and Mantra...

You possess a strong drive for ambition, and are not afraid to jump in headfirst to pursue your goals. However, at times, this may result in impulsive or forced actions. You have received a quality education, and possess confidence in your communication skills.

Mantra   "I take bold and decisive action, communicating clearly and confidently. I embrace change and am always willing to explore new ideas and perspectives. I trust my instincts and make decisions with purpose and clarity.

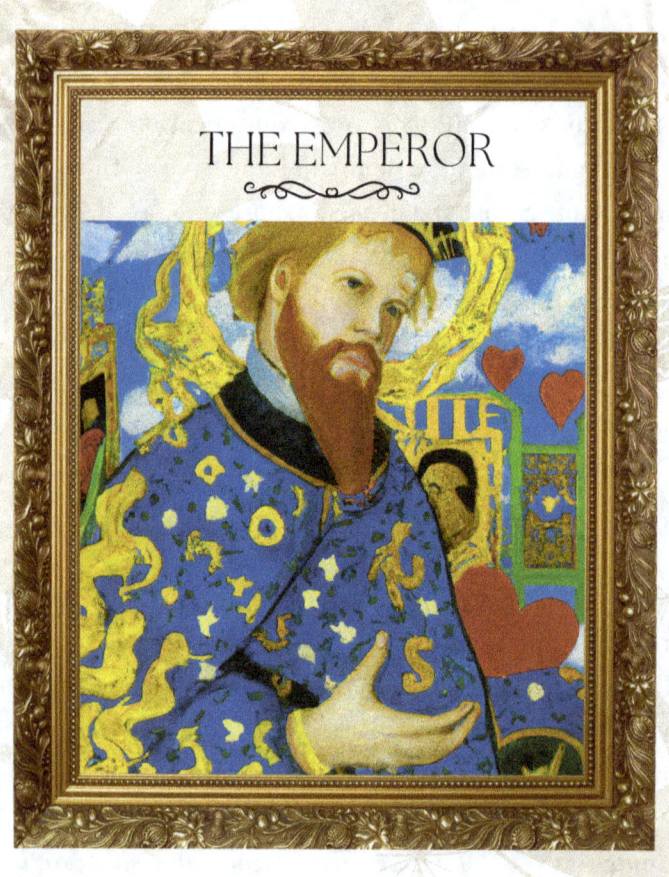

The card the guides have chosen for you is...

The Tarot "The Emperor" represents authority, structure, and stability. It symbolizes a mature, responsible, and confident individual who is in control of their life and surroundings. The Emperor is often depicted as a king or ruler, sitting on his throne, holding a scepter, and wearing a crown. The Emperor represents a need for control, order, and discipline, both in one's personal life and in relationships with others. When The Emperor appears in a reading, it may indicate a desire for stability and security, or a need to establish boundaries and take charge. It may also suggest that one should take a leadership role, be more assertive, or make decisions based on reason and logic. Overall, The Emperor is a reminder of the importance of taking control of one's life and asserting oneself in a confident and decisive manner.

Interpretation and Mantra...

You're creating frameworks and bases that will serve as the groundwork for your achievements. You prioritize stability and assurance over adaptability and modification. You possess the determination to stick to your plans until they are completed.

Mantra "I am in control. I am assertive and confident. I am a leader, making decisions based on reason and logic."

PAGE OF PENTACLES

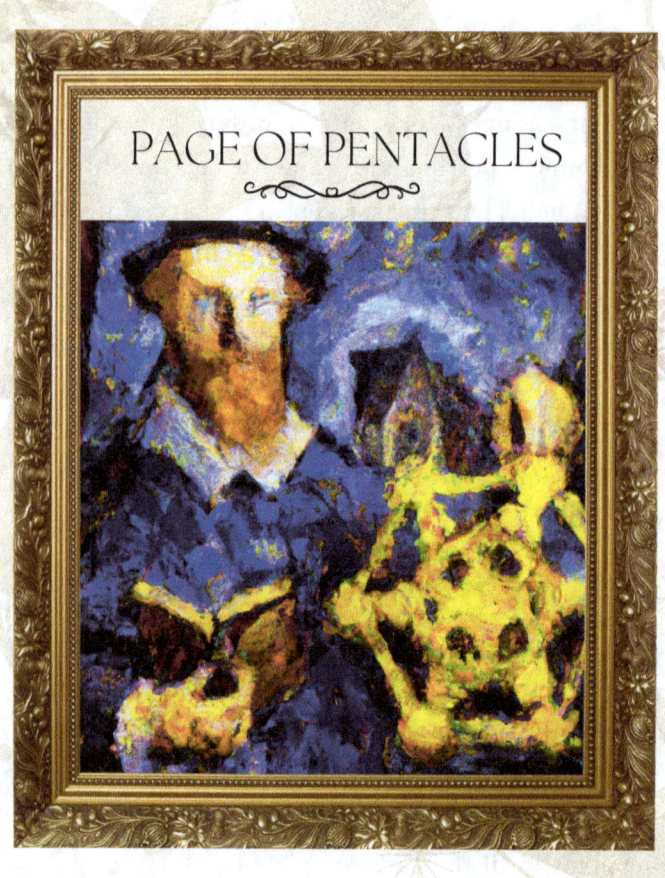

The card the guides have chosen for you is...

The tarot, Page of Pentacles represents new beginnings, growth, and potential. It is associated with the earth element, which represents stability, abundance, and material prosperity. The Page of Pentacles symbolizes a time of learning, growth, and exploration. It may indicate a new opportunity or a fresh start, especially in the areas of money, work, or education. Page of Pentacles suggests a period of hard work and dedication, where you are willing to invest time and effort into achieving your goals. The Page of Pentacles may also represent someone in your life who is diligent, practical, and responsible. It is a reminder to stay focused on your goals and to work hard to bring your dreams to reality. The Page of Pentacles suggests that it's a time for developing your skills, building a solid foundation, and laying the groundwork for future success.

Interpretation and Mantra...

You are motivated to pursue a fresh financial or career prospect, and you recognize the possibility of expanding and achieving your objectives. You are prepared to enhance your abilities and acquire knowledge in a new area.

Mantra "I embrace new opportunities and invest in my growth. I am dedicated to building a solid foundation for my future success."

PAGE OF WANDS

The card the guides have chosen for you is...

The Page of Wands is a tarot that represents new beginnings, inspiration, and creativity. It can indicate that you are about to embark on a new journey or project, and it is a sign that you should be open to new ideas and possibilities. The Page of Wands is also associated with communication and self-expression, so it may be a sign that you need to speak up and share your thoughts and ideas with others. The Page of Wands can also indicate that you are feeling confident and excited about the future. Overall, the Page of Wands is a positive and encouraging card that suggests that you should have faith in yourself and your abilities, and that new opportunities are on the horizon.

Interpretation and Mantra...

You have a free-spirited nature and a zeal for life. Your mind is brimming with fresh concepts, which is causing a sense of creative restlessness. You sense a strong urge to utilize these ideas to initiate a new chapter of your life, perhaps even in a spiritual direction.

Mantra "I am open to new ideas and opportunities, I trust in my abilities and I am ready to take action towards my goals."

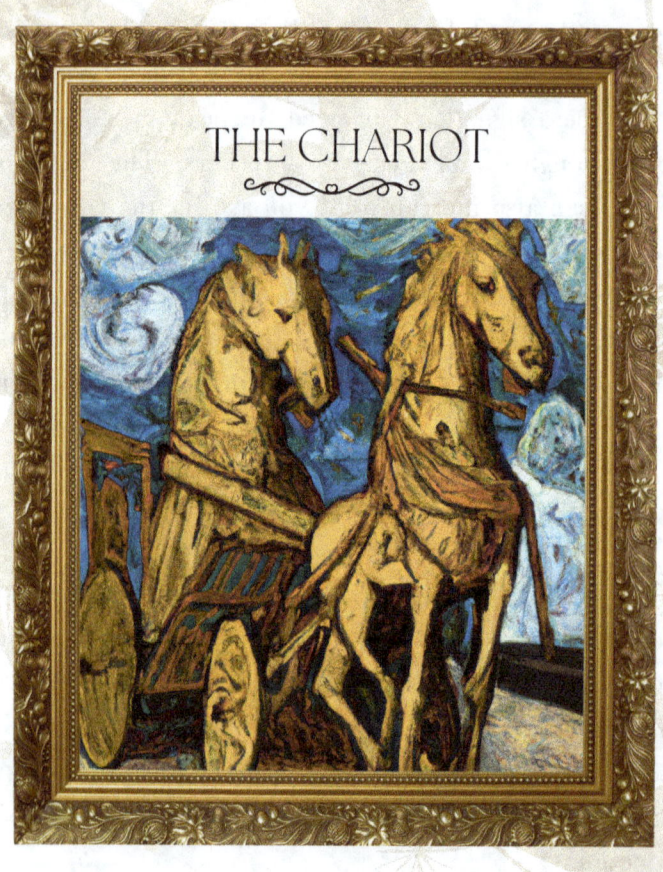

The card the guides have chosen for you is...

The Chariot represents victory and triumph through determination and control. It is associated with the astrological sign of Cancer and is often interpreted as a sign of a journey or a major change in one's life. The Chariot usually depicts a figure in armor, sitting in a chariot pulled by two sphinxes or horses. The figure holds the reins, representing control and the power to steer one's own destiny. The Chariot can also represent the balance between the conflicting forces of the conscious and unconscious mind, and the ability to harness them in order to achieve one's goals. It is a powerful card that advises to stay focused on your goal and not to lose control of your emotions and actions.

Interpretation and Mantra...

You are a potent impetus, propelled by fortitude and unwavering determination. You spare no effort in your pursuit of success, surmounting obstacles and harmonizing divergent forces along the way.

Mantra "I am in control of my destiny and I will triumph through determination and focus."

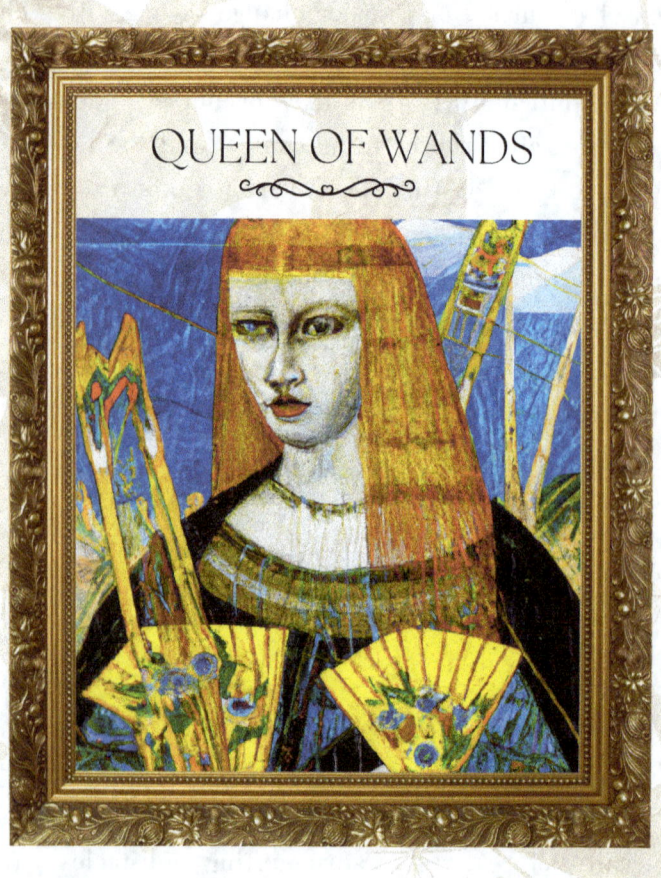

The card the guides have chosen for you is...

The Queen of Wands tarot symbolizes creativity, confidence, and determination. She is often depicted holding a wand, which represents her energetic and pioneering spirit. She represents a strong-willed and independent woman who is driven and knows what she wants. She is a natural leader, able to inspire and motivate others with her vision and enthusiasm. The Queen of Wands is associated with the element of fire, which represents passion, motivation, and creativity. The Queen of Wands often appears in a reading as a sign of success, especially in career and business matters, as well as a signal to embrace new opportunities and take bold steps forward. Overall, the Queen of Wands represents a powerful and dynamic force that encourages one to trust their intuition and follow their dreams.

Interpretation and Mantra...

With your active social life, you lead a bustling existence, forging relationships with others and boldly pursuing your creative aspirations. Your self-assuredness, bravery, and tenacity allow you to fearlessly assert your opinions and make your voice heard.

Mantra "I am confident and fearless, I trust in my passions and ideas, and I bring my fiery energy to every pursuit I undertake."

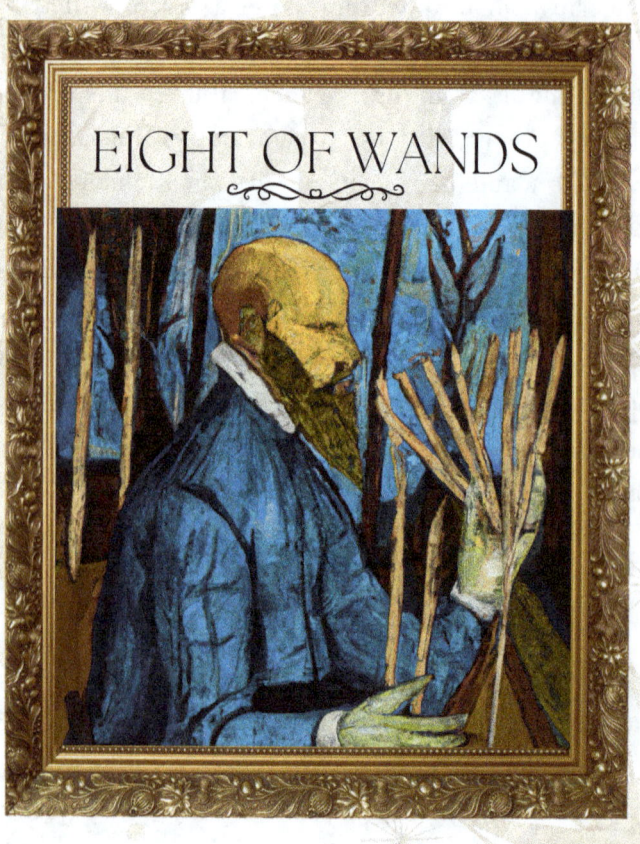

The card the guides have chosen for you is...

The Eight of Wands in a tarot reading can indicate movement and swift action. It often represents communication and messages, indicating that news or information is on its way and decisions will need to be made quickly. It can also suggest travel and changes in plans or direction. In a career or business context, the Eight of Wands can indicate success and progress, but also a need to stay flexible and adapt to new developments. In a relationship, the Eight of Wands can suggest a sense of excitement and passion, but also the need to work through any obstacles that may arise. The eight wands in the image are usually moving swiftly and in perfect coordination, which symbolizes a sense of harmony and balance in the midst of change and movement. Eight of Wands can also indicate that a new beginning or opportunity is on the horizon and it is time to take action to seize it.

Interpretation and Mantra...

At present, everything is happening at a rapid pace. Embrace the current momentum and utilize it to drive favorable transformation and achieve significant outcomes. Additionally, travel may be on the horizon for you.

Mantra: "I am openhearted to new and positive changes."

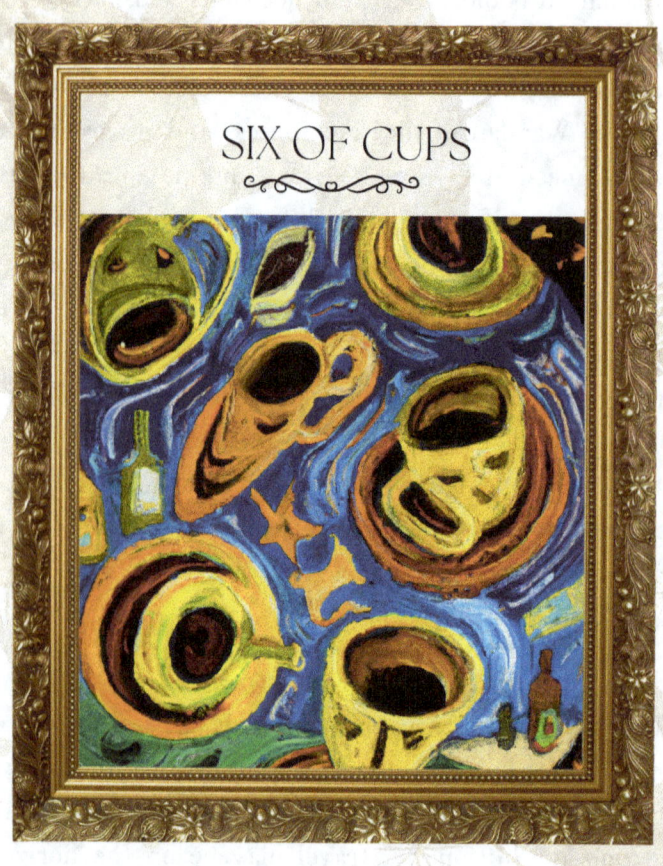

The card the guides have chosen for you is...

The Six of Cups represents nostalgia, childhood memories, and emotional healing. It is associated with the water element, which represents emotions and feelings. The Six of Cups symbolizes a time of looking back on the past, recalling fond memories, and reconnecting with old friends or loved ones. This card may indicate a return to a simpler, more innocent time in your life, and a desire to recapture that sense of security and comfort. The Six of Cups can also suggest a time of healing and emotional renewal, where you are able to let go of past hurts and move forward in a more positive direction. It is a reminder to nurture your inner child, to reconnect with your emotions, and to find comfort and joy in the simple things in life. The Six of Cups suggests that it's a time for emotional healing and for letting go of the past in order to move forward in a more positive direction.

Interpretation and Mantra...

You are enveloped in joyful recollections from the past, such as reconnecting with childhood pals or former flames. You experience a sense of lightheartedness and creativity. You foster unity and teamwork in your present relationships.

Mantra "I embrace my memories, heal my emotions, and move forward with joy."

The card the guides have chosen for you is...

The Queen of Swords is from the Minor Arcana in a tarot deck. The Queen of Swords represents the qualities of intelligence, clear thinking, and communication. She is a highly analytical and logical person, who is able to cut through illusions and see things as they truly are. She is a truthful and direct person, who speaks her mind without fear or hesitation. Queen of Swords can indicate that a person is able to think objectively and make decisions based on reason and evidence, rather than emotions. It can also suggest that a person is able to communicate effectively and persuasively, and that they are able to convey their ideas and opinions clearly and concisely. In a reading, the Queen of Swords can be a sign of clear thinking, rationality, and good decision making, and it encourages the person to trust their intellect and to communicate effectively.

Interpretation and Mantra...

You are resolute, tenacious, and astute. You prioritize rational thinking over emotional responses. You have zero tolerance for falsehoods or unnecessary embellishments. You are known for your directness and consequently, many people value your viewpoint.

Mantra "*I think clearly, speak my truth and make wise decisions.*"

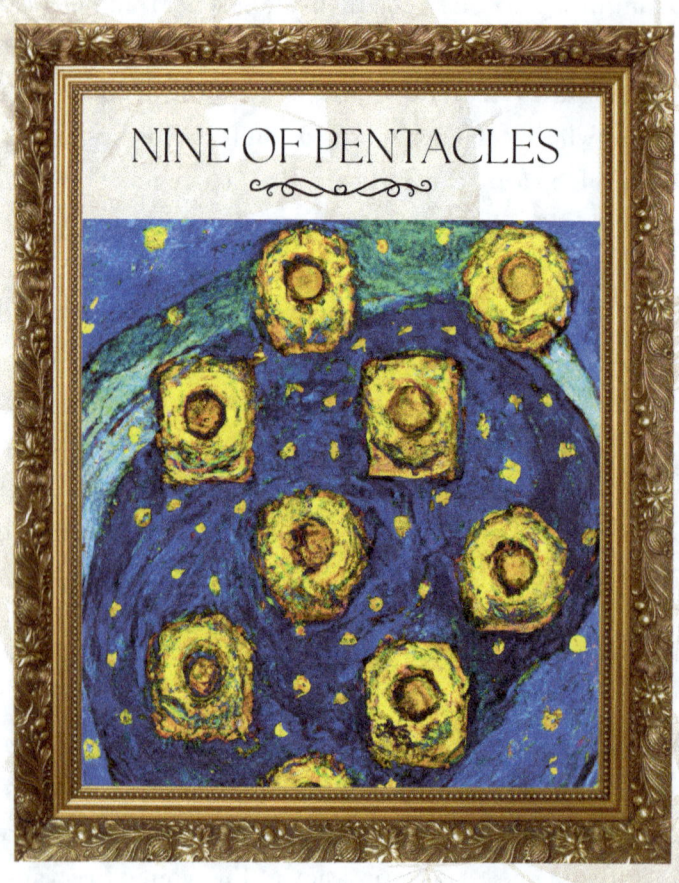

The card the guides have chosen for you is...

The tarot Nine of Pentacles represents a time of satisfaction and contentment, often symbolizing self-sufficiency, comfort, and stability. Nine of Pentacles suggests that you are reaping the rewards of your hard work and are enjoying the fruits of your labor. It can indicate financial stability, independence, and luxury. On a deeper level, the Nine of Pentacles may represent a time of self-discovery, where you are able to appreciate your own talents and abilities. This may also indicate that you are taking care of yourself, both physically and emotionally. Overall, the Nine of Pentacles is a positive and uplifting card that represents a time of personal growth and self-fulfillment.

Interpretation and Mantra...

You have successfully generated abundance, and it's time to relish the fruits of your labor. Treat yourself to something indulgent without hesitation. Additionally, leverage your prosperity to create long-term financial independence.

Mantra   "*I am self-sufficient, I am confident and proud, I enjoy the fruits of my labor and nurture myself both inside and out.*"

SEVEN OF PENTACLES

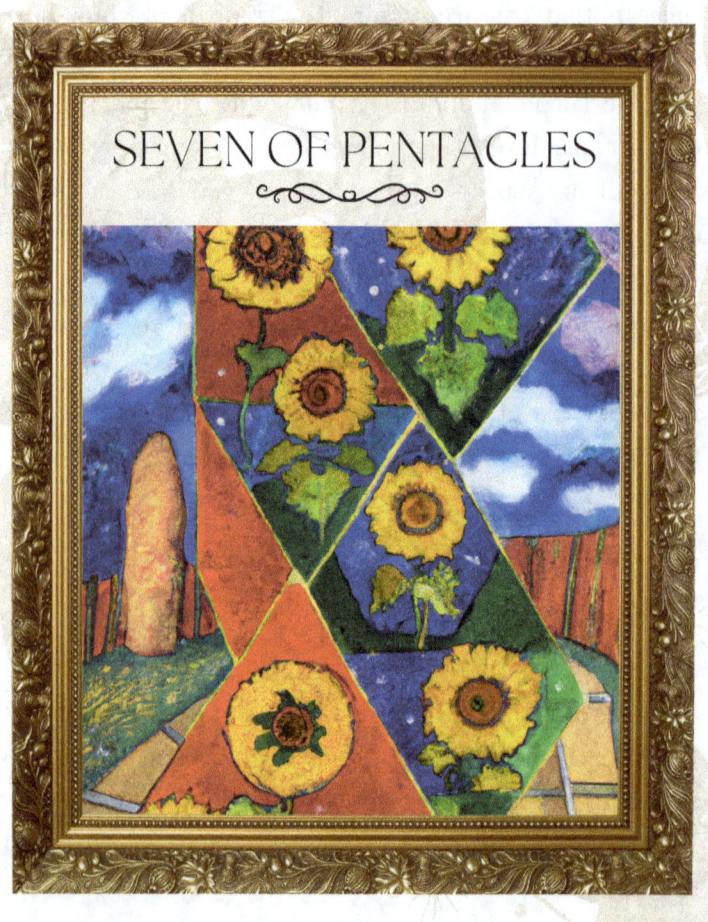

The card the guides have chosen for you is...

The Seven of Pentacles tarot represents a time of reflection and reassessment. It symbolizes a moment of pause, where one takes stock of their efforts and evaluates their progress towards their goals. The image often depicts a gardener examining his crops, symbolizing the need to assess and evaluate one's hard work and investment. The Seven of Pentacles represents a time to reflect on one's progress and determine what changes need to be made to move forward. This can indicate a time of self-reflection and introspection, where one takes a step back to consider their direction and make any necessary adjustments. It can also suggest a need to balance a focus on progress with patience and persistence. The Seven of Pentacles tarot is a powerful symbol of reflection, reassessment, and introspection.

Interpretation and Mantra...

You are willing to put in the necessary effort now, understanding that the fruits of your labor may not be immediately visible. You recognize that success is a long-term endeavor and are willing to exercise patience while awaiting the rewards. Having done what you can, you now await the pay-off with diligence.

Mantra "*I take time to reflect on my progress and reassess my efforts. I balance my focus on progress with patience and persistence.*"

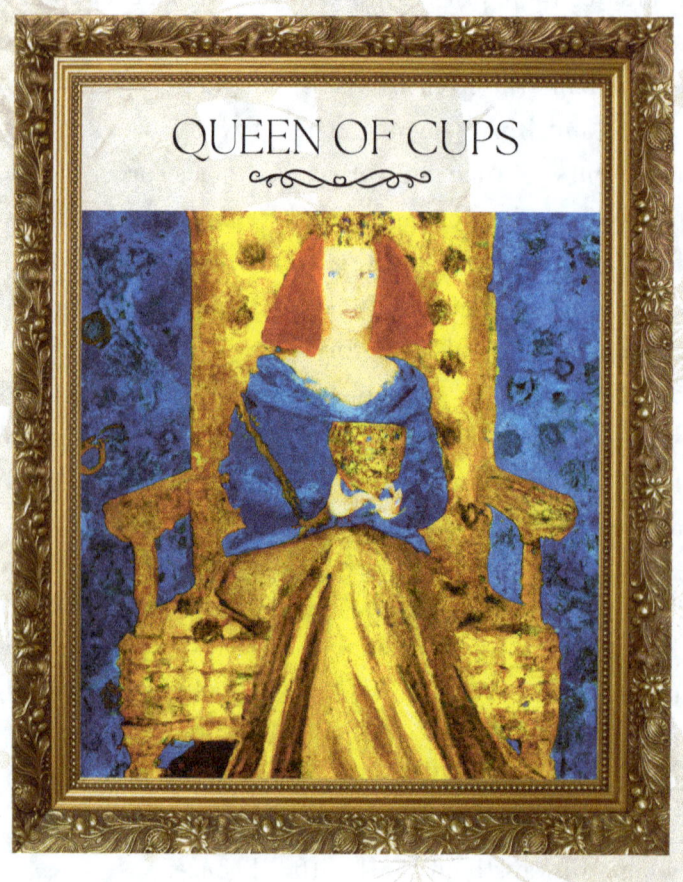

The card the guides have chosen for you is...

The Queen of Cups tarot represents compassion, empathy, and emotional intelligence. It symbolizes a time of sensitivity and nurturing, often reflecting a deep understanding of others' feelings and needs. The image often depicts a queen holding a cup, symbolizing the ability to nurture and care for others. The Queen of Cups represents a desire to comfort and support those around you, leveraging your emotional intelligence to create a sense of connection and understanding. This can indicate a time of deep introspection and reflection, where one takes stock of their emotions and navigates their relationships with care and compassion. It can also suggest a need to balance a focus on emotions with a sense of practicality and stability. The Queen of Cups tarot is a powerful symbol of compassion, empathy, and emotional intelligence

Interpretation and Mantra...

You embody the qualities of a nurturer and a mother figure, offering support to others through active listening, deep compassion, and a genuine care for their wellbeing. Your heightened intuition and creativity enable you to tap into the energies surrounding you, allowing you to move in a state of effortless flow.

Mantra *"I nurture and care for others with compassion and empathy. I balance my emotions with a sense of practicality and stability."*

THE HERMIT

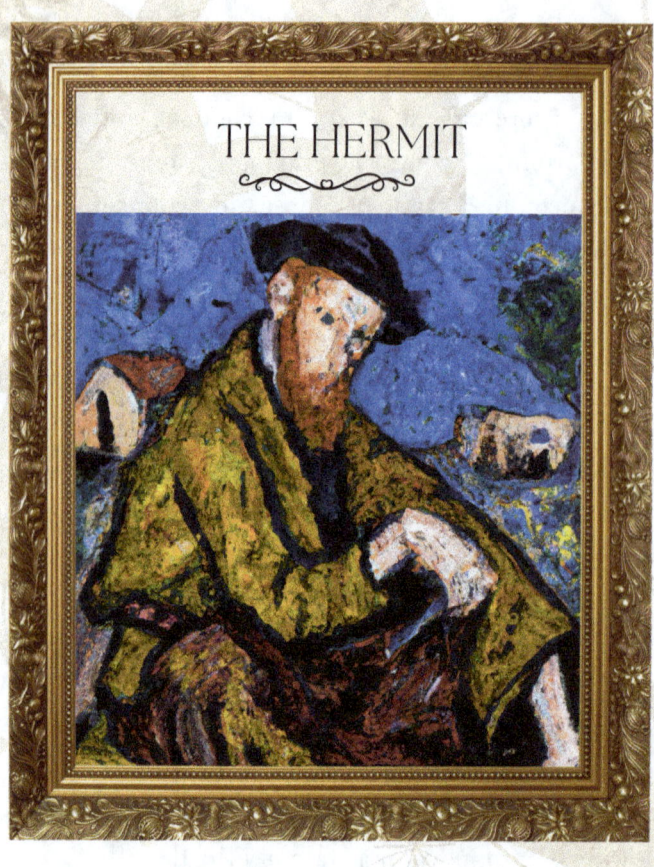

The card the guides have chosen for you is...

The Hermit represents introspection, wisdom, and solitude. It is associated with the earth element, which represents stability and material abundance. The Hermit symbolizes a time of introspection, reflection, and contemplation. This Hermit may indicate that you are in need of some time alone, to think, reflect, and gain greater understanding and insight into your life and your experiences. The Hermit can also suggest that you are seeking answers, knowledge, and wisdom, and that you are looking within yourself for guidance and understanding. It is a reminder to take time for introspection, to seek knowledge and wisdom through quiet reflection, and to trust your own inner guidance. The Hermit suggests that it's a time for seeking answers within yourself, for reflecting on your experiences, and for gaining a deeper understanding of your life and your place in the world.

Interpretation and Mantra...

You are following a journey of spiritual enlightenment and personal exploration. Step away from your everyday routine and establish a space for self-reflection. Turn inward and you will unveil the wisdom and understanding you are seeking.

Mantra   *"I seek knowledge, wisdom, and understanding through introspection and reflection."*

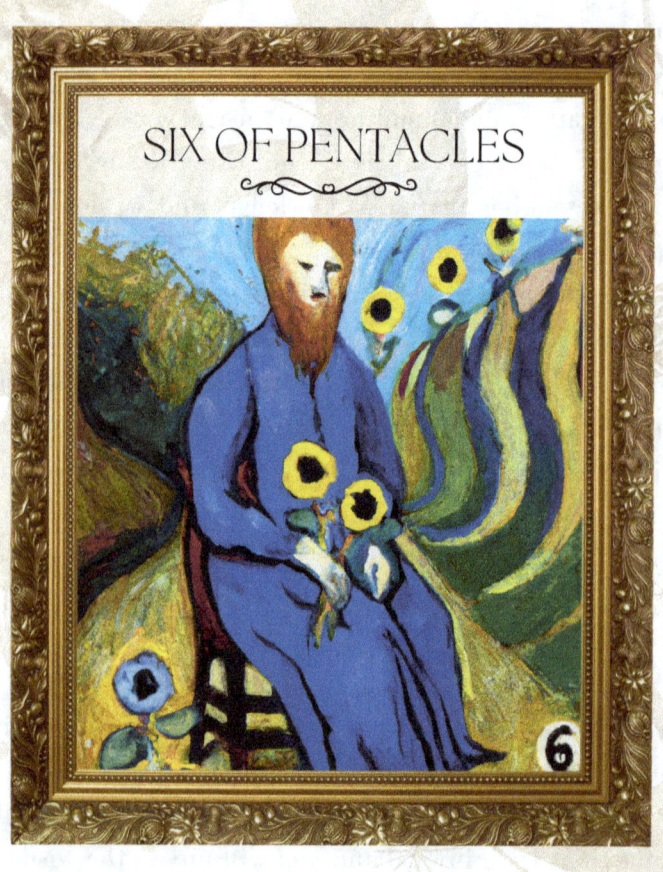

The card the guides have chosen for you is...

The Tarot Six of Pentacles represents a time of balance and fairness. It often symbolizes giving and receiving, charity, and the idea of "what goes around comes around". This would suggest that you may be in a position to help others, or that you are receiving help from someone else. It can indicate a time of generosity and mutual support, where you are able to give and receive freely without feeling weighed down. On a deeper level, the Six of Pentacles may represent a time of spiritual growth, where you are able to connect with your inner self and understand your own needs and desires. It can also indicate that you are learning how to balance your own wants and needs with those of others, creating a harmonious and fulfilling life.

Interpretation and Mantra...

You are in a generous spirit and eager to share your abundance and wealth with others. Alternatively, you may find yourself on the receiving end of someone's generosity, accepting their gifts with gratitude. Remember to give generously, as it is believed that it will return to you threefold.

Mantra   "*I balance giving and receiving, creating harmony in my relationships and with the world.*"

JUSTICE

The card the guides have chosen for you is...

The tarot Justice represents balance, fairness, and decision-making. It is a sign of legal matters and signifies that the querent will receive a fair judgment. Justice is associated with the astrological sign of Libra, which is also associated with balance and harmony. This can represent a situation where the querent will be called upon to make an important decision or judgment, and they are encouraged to weigh all options carefully before making a choice. Justice also represents the consequences of one's actions, and it is a reminder that what goes around comes around. In a reading, Justice can indicate that the querent will find resolution and closure in a difficult situation, or that they will receive the rewards or consequences for their actions. Overall, Justice is a reminder to be fair, just and honest in all our actions, and to be prepared to accept the consequences of our decisions.

Interpretation and Mantra...

You comprehend the relationship between actions and their repercussions, and recognize that your decisions carry consequences. You endeavor to create equity and equilibrium, striving for the most equitable resolution for everyone involved.

Mantra "I seek balance and fairness in all things. I make my decisions with integrity and impartiality. I am ready to accept the consequences of my actions. Justice guide me on my path."

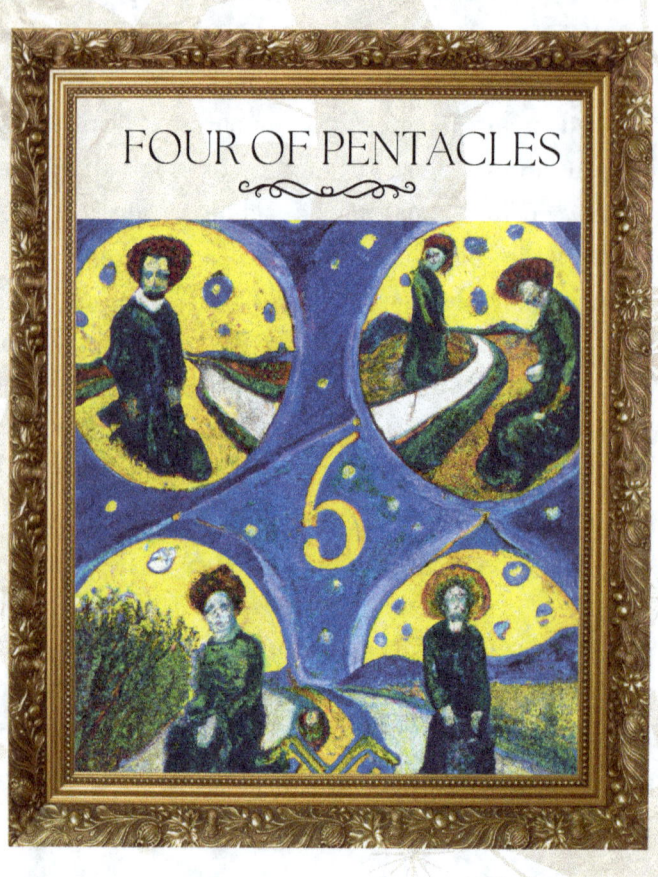

The card the guides have chosen for you is...

The Tarot Four of Pentacles represents stability, security, and control. It symbolizes a focus on material possessions, wealth, and power. The image often shows a figure clutching tightly to one or more pentacles, representing a desire to hold onto what they have and maintain control over their resources. This can indicate a need for stability and security, and a focus on accumulating wealth and material possessions. However, it can also suggest a tendency to be overly possessive and greedy, leading to a feeling of isolation and a lack of connection with others. When Four of Pentacles appears in a reading, it may indicate a need to strike a balance between holding onto what is valuable and allowing for a healthy flow of resources and generosity. It may also suggest the importance of finding contentment and security from within, rather than relying solely on external possessions.

Interpretation and Mantra...

You are extremely mindful of your finances, consistently setting aside funds and monitoring your expenditures. However, it is important to remember that money thrives when it is circulating and being exchanged, rather than when it is being hoarded or saved excessively.

Mantra "I balance my desire for stability and security with generosity and openness."

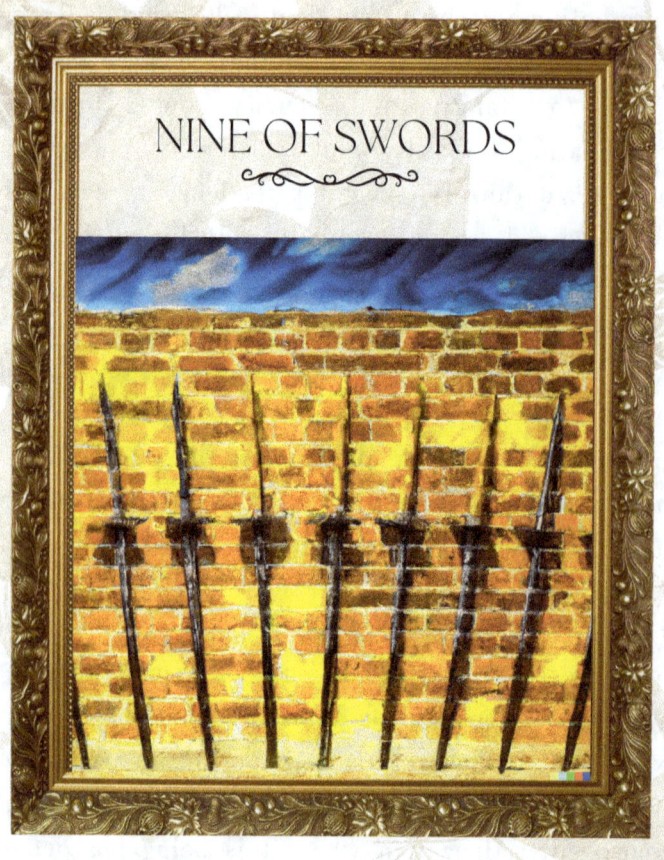

The card the guides have chosen for you is...

The Nine of Swords represents fear, anxiety, and nightmares. It often appears when one is consumed by negative thoughts and worries. It can also indicate feelings of guilt and regret. However, the Nine of Swords is not just about negative emotions. It's also about the power of the mind and how our thoughts shape our reality. The Nine of Swords encourages us to face our fears, confront our anxieties, and turn them into positive experiences. It's a reminder that we have the power to overcome our inner demons and to take control of our thoughts. By doing so, we can transform our lives and find peace of mind.

Interpretation and Mantra...

You are struggling with gloomy thoughts and unsettling emotions. Worry, despair, and anxiety may be causing sleepless nights. It's important to avoid getting too involved with your fears, as this may lead them to dominate your life. Reach out to someone for assistance.

Mantra "I face my fears and embrace my inner strength. I release my anxieties and transform them into peace. I take control of my thoughts and find solace in the present moment."

THE WORLD

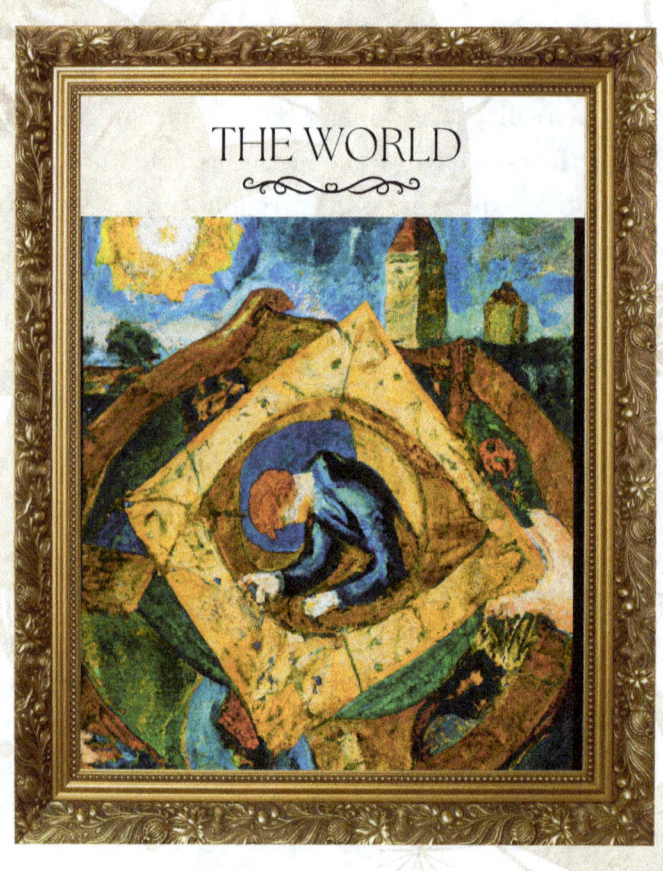

The card the guides have chosen for you is...

The World tarot symbolizes completion, fulfillment, and a sense of satisfaction with one's journey through life. The World tarot represents a time of celebration, where one can look back on their accomplishments with pride and look forward to a future filled with potential and possibility.

This can indicate a time of travel, both physical and spiritual, where one is able to expand their horizons and explore new places, ideas, and experiences. The World tarot also symbolizes a sense of unity, where one is able to see the interconnectedness of all things and understand their place in the larger picture. Whether you are looking to bring a sense of closure to a project, celebrate your achievements, or simply find a sense of peace and fulfillment in your life, the World tarot is a powerful reminder of the potential for completion and the joy of celebrating one's journey through life.

Interpretation and Mantra...

You have completed a significant project or phase, and are now celebrating a full circle moment. As one chapter comes to a close, another opens up for you.

Mantra "I am at peace with my journey and embrace the world around me."

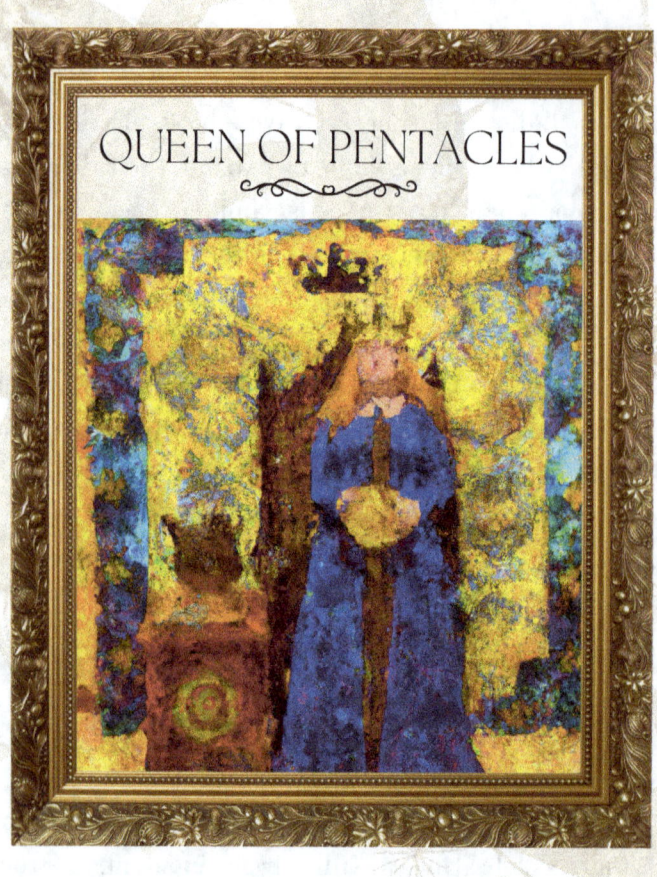

The card the guides have chosen for you is...

The Queen of Pentacles tarot represents practicality, comfort, and abundance. She symbolizes nurturing and taking care of oneself and others, and often reflects a time of stability and comfort. The Queen of Pentacles is depicted with a bounty of fruits and flowers, reflecting her abundance and prosperity. This often suggests a focus on stability and security in one's personal and financial life. The Queen of Pentacles can also indicate a strong work ethic and the ability to manifest one's goals into reality. It often represents a caregiver and nurturer, who is able to provide comfort and security to those around her. However, it can also indicate a need for balance, as too much focus on material wealth and comfort can lead to neglect of other important aspects of life. The Queen of Pentacles tarot is a powerful symbol of abundance, comfort, and practicality.

Interpretation and Mantra...

You are an exemplary parent who manages both family and work responsibilities with skill and grace. You balance your domestic obligations with your career goals and financial aspirations, creating a harmonious equilibrium in your life.

Mantra "I am abundant and prosperous in all areas of my life. I nurture and care for myself and others, creating comfort and stability."

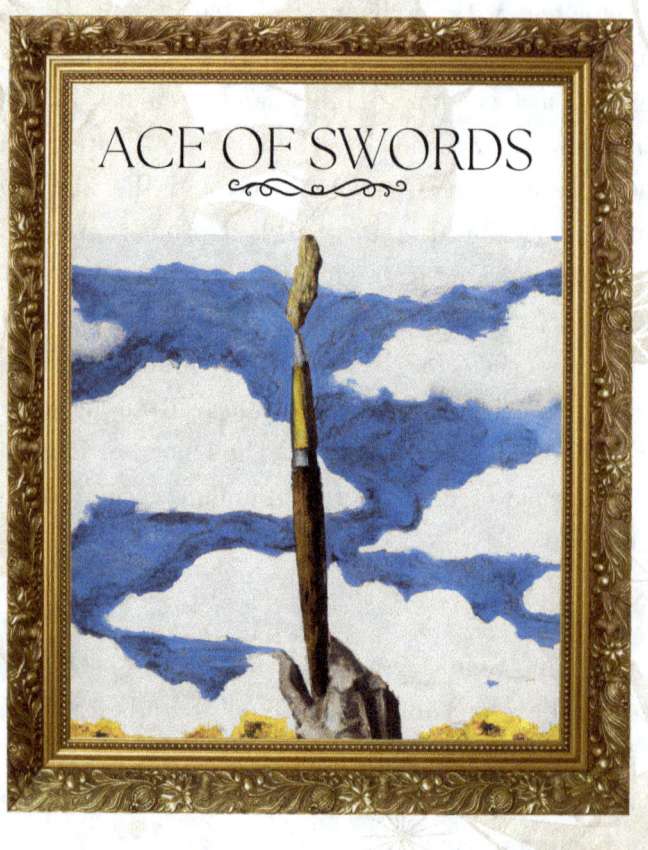

The card the guides have chosen for you is...

The Ace of Swords represents the beginning of a new mental or intellectual journey. It is associated with the element of air and the power of the mind. The imagery on the card typically depicts a sword or a hand holding a sword, which is a symbol of clarity, precision, and power of the mind. This card can indicate the start of a new idea or project, a new perspective, or a new way of thinking.

The Ace of Swords suggests that the querent is about to experience a breakthrough in their thinking, or a new understanding of a situation. It can indicate the ability to make a clear and decisive decision, or the ability to cut through confusion and uncertainty. The card can also indicate the power of communication, and the ability to express oneself clearly and persuasively. This card can be a sign of mental acuity and the ability to see through illusions and deceptions.

When reversed, the Ace of Swords can indicate a blockage in the mental realm, such as a lack of clarity or a fear of facing the truth. It may also indicate a lack of communication or a lack of mental focus. Overall, the Ace of Swords is a powerful card that represents the ability to think clearly and make decisions with confidence.

Interpretation and Mantra...

You are experiencing a breakthrough and a new way of thinking. Your mind is stretched by new ideas and you are excited about putting those ideas into action.

Mantra: "I think clearly and trust my own judgment."

The card the guides have chosen for you is...

The Five of Swords tarot represents defeat, loss and feelings of being overpowered. This can indicate a situation where one person has taken advantage of another, leaving the victim feeling betrayed and defeated. It can also indicate a situation where a person has experienced a loss or defeat and is now facing feelings of shame and self-doubt. The swords in the card symbolize conflict and the number five can indicate changes and instability. The overall meaning of the Five of Swords suggests that the situation is not in your favor and it may be time to accept defeat and move on, rather than continue to fight a losing battle. It may be wise to consider seeking help from others and finding a new approach to the situation.

Interpretation and Mantra...

You have been entangled in a situation where someone has to win and someone has to lose. The trust between you and others has been ruptured, and you feel like you're in competition rather than cooperation. To move forward, try to find common ground or seek forgiveness..

Mantra "I surrender my struggles and trust in the journey ahead. I choose to release my attachment to past defeats and embrace the opportunities for growth and transformation."

THE EMPRESS

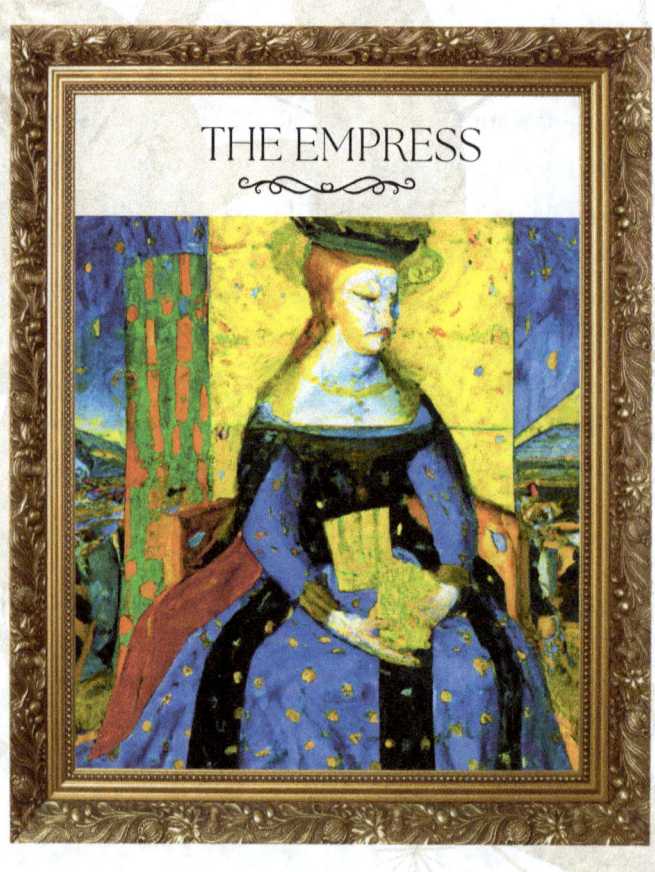

The card the guides have chosen for you is...

The Empress tarot represents nurturing, motherhood, and femininity. The Empress indicates that the querent is in a time of growth and creation, and it suggests a feeling of abundance and fertility. The Empress also represents the ability to manifest abundance and to create the life that you want. It can indicate that the querent is in a time of abundance, whether that be financial, emotional or in terms of love and relationships. In a negative context, it may indicate that the querent is too focused on material possessions and neglecting their emotional needs. Overall, the Empress is a reminder to nurture yourself and your relationships, to focus on growth and creation, and to manifest abundance in all areas of life.

Interpretation and Mantra...

You are receiving an abundance of creative energy. You are embodying the mother archetype and birthing a new project into being. Your divine feminine energy is flowing through you as you grow and nurture your creation.

Mantra "I nurture myself and my relationships, manifesting abundance and focusing on growth and creation in all areas of my life."

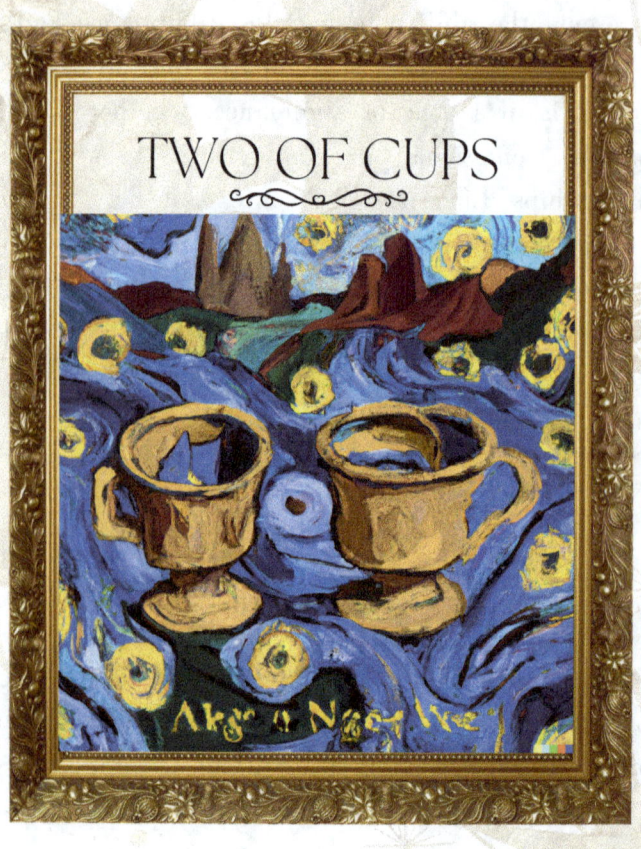

The card the guides have chosen for you is...

The Two of Cups represents the union of two people or forces. It is often associated with love and relationships, and can indicate the beginning of a romantic partnership or the deepening of an existing one. The imagery typically depicts two people, often a man and a woman, sharing a cup in a gesture of unity and harmony. It can also represent a balance of masculine and feminine energies, or the coming together of different aspects of the self. In a reading, the Two of Cups suggests that the querent is ready to open their heart and form a connection with another person or aspect of themselves. It can indicate a time of emotional fulfillment and happiness, and a strong sense of mutual understanding and support. The Two of Cups can also indicate a strong emotional bond, whether it is romantic or platonic.

In a more general sense, the Two of Cups can also indicate a balance and harmony in other areas of life, such as in business or creative endeavors. It can be a sign of a successful collaboration, or a mutually beneficial agreement.

Interpretation and Mantra...

You are establishing a profound alliance founded on mutual values, empathy, and unconditional affection. You perceive the divine essence in others. Foster these fresh relationships since they bear promise for the future.

Mantra: "I am now ready to let love into my life..

TEN OF WANDS

The card the guides have chosen for you is...

The Ten of Wands represents the feeling of being overwhelmed and burdened. It suggests that you may be carrying too many responsibilities and tasks on your shoulders, leading to exhaustion and burnout. This warns against taking on too much, and encourages you to reassess your priorities and delegate tasks if necessary. It also suggests that you may be feeling weighed down by your own self-imposed expectations and the pressure to succeed. The Ten of Wands reminds you to pace yourself and not to forget to take care of yourself. By letting go of some of the burden and finding a balance, you can rediscover joy and fulfillment in your pursuits.

Interpretation and Mantra...

You are willingly shouldering additional burdens, workloads, and responsibilities. While you recognize that it's only temporary, you're prepared to put in the effort now to achieve your objective and reap the benefits in the future.

Mantra "I release the weight and embrace clarity. I trust in my abilities to overcome challenges and find balance."

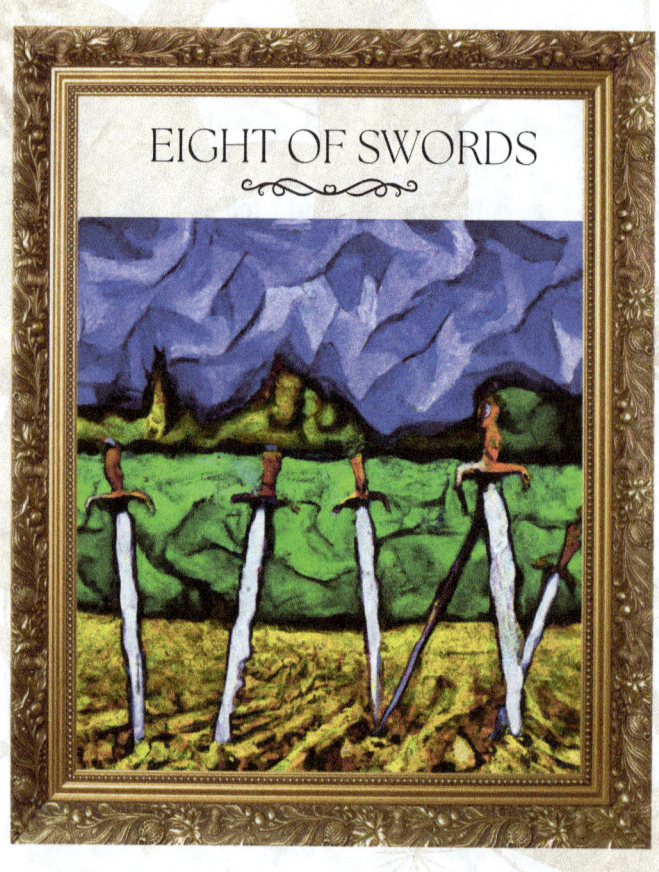

The card the guides have chosen for you is...

The Eight of Swords represents feeling trapped, limited, and powerless. It is associated with the astrological sign of Gemini and it usually depicts a woman bound and blindfolded, surrounded by eight swords. This symbolizes the feeling of being trapped in a difficult or confusing situation, and feeling unable to move forward. It can also represent feeling limited by one's own thoughts and beliefs.

The Eight of Swords can indicate that the querent may be feeling trapped in a cycle of negative thoughts and self-doubt and that they are unable to see the full picture of their situation.

However, the Eight of Swords also carries a message of hope. It is a reminder that the querent has the power to break free from their own limitations and to take control of their thoughts and emotions.

Interpretation and Mantra...

You feel trapped by your thoughts and your situation, and you believe you are the victim. While it may appear as if you have few choices, the bindings around you are loose and if you change your thoughts you will change your life.

Mantra "I break free from my self-imposed limitations, I trust in my own strength and abilities. I see the truth and I am empowered."

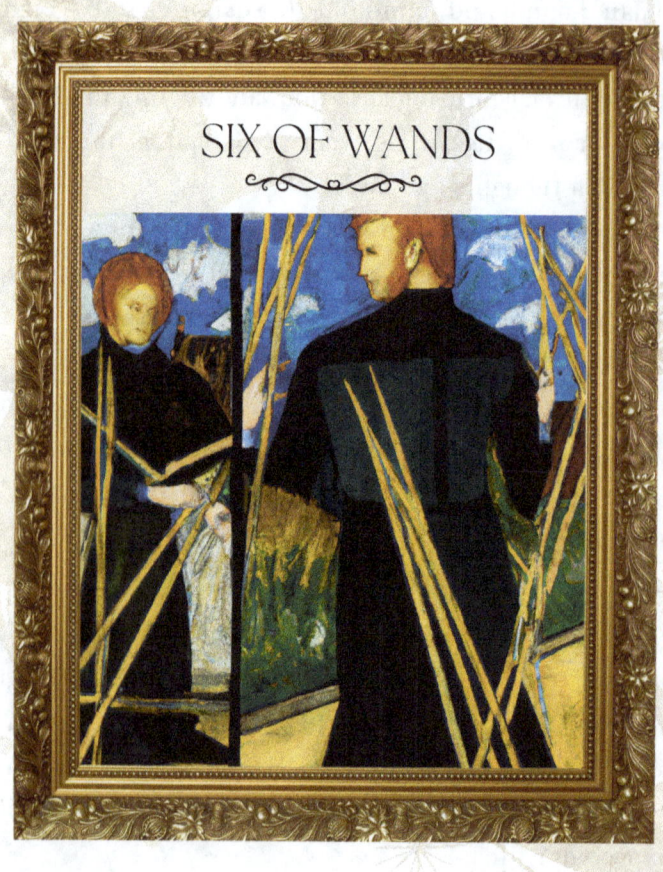

The card the guides have chosen for you is...

The Tarot the Six of Wands represents victory, success, and recognition. It symbolizes the triumph of the individual over obstacles and challenges and is a clear indication of the rewards of hard work and determination. The usual image is of a rider on a horse carrying a banner is a symbol of celebration and recognition for one's achievements. This suggests a feeling of pride, confidence, and satisfaction and is often seen as a sign of success in personal and professional matters. The Six of Wands also suggests that others may look to the individual for guidance and inspiration and may represent the rewards of leadership and taking charge. Six of Swords can be a source of encouragement and motivation, reminding us to strive for success and to never give up on our goals.

Interpretation and Mantra...

You are filled with confidence, self-assurance, and a sense of achievement. You take pride in your accomplishments and are eager to share them with others. Your success is acknowledged by those around you who offer their support and encouragement.

Mantra "I am victorious and proud. I embrace success and recognition for my hard work and determination"

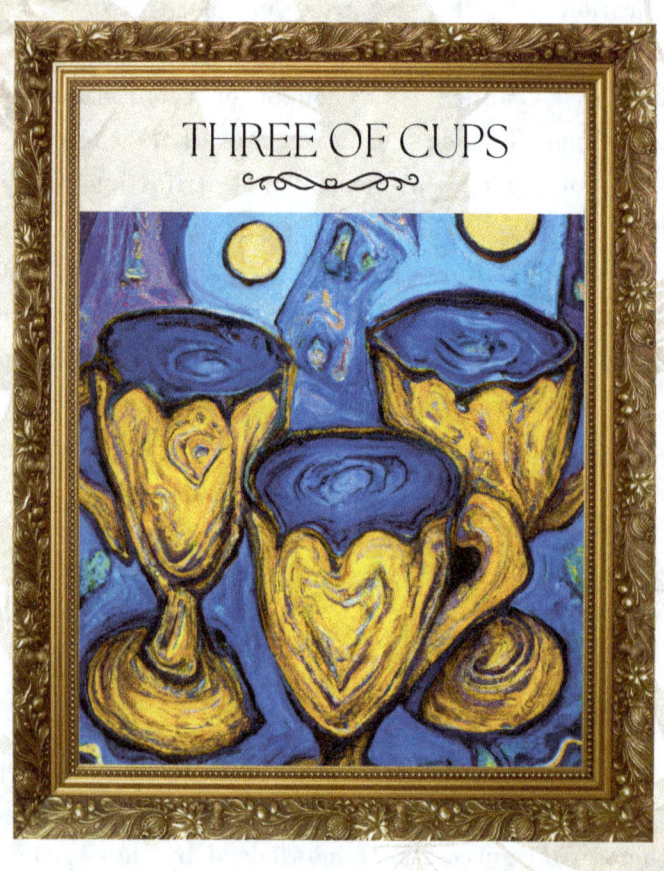

The card the guides have chosen for you is...

The Three of Cups in a tarot reading represents celebration, joy, and friendship. This card can indicate that the querent is surrounded by loved ones and is enjoying a time of celebration and happiness. It suggests a sense of community and a feeling of belonging. The Three of Cups also represents emotional fulfillment and a sense of harmony in relationships. It can indicate that the querent is experiencing a time of emotional abundance and that they are surrounded by people who care for them. In a negative context, it may indicate a lack of balance and overindulgence. Overall, the Three of Cups is a reminder to appreciate the people in your life and to take the time to celebrate and enjoy the good things that you have.

Interpretation and Mantra...

Mark your achievements by sharing them with your dearest friends and family. Work jointly with others on a innovative venture and encourage each other to attain greater goals.

Mantra "I celebrate and cherish the joys and friendships in my life, embracing emotional fulfillment and harmony."

The card the guides have chosen for you is...

The Tarot Four of Wands symbolizes celebration, peace, and harmony. It is often associated with gatherings, parties, and events that bring people together. The Four of Wands represents a time of joy and satisfaction, where all your hard work and effort have finally paid off. The Four of Wands is a sign of stability and security, indicating that you can now relax and enjoy the fruits of your labors. The image usually features four wands forming an arch, under which people are dancing and celebrating. Four of Wands is a reminder to take a break and enjoy the moment, to celebrate your accomplishments and look forward to a bright future. The Four of Wands suggests that everything is going well in your life and that you should continue to build on your success.

Interpretation and Mantra...

After experiencing rapid growth and expansion, it's crucial to take a break and acknowledge your accomplishments. Take pleasure in the rewards of your hard work. Additionally, a wedding, birthday, reunion, or family gathering might be on the horizon.

Mantra "I celebrate my achievements and enjoy the moment. I am surrounded by peace, harmony, and joy."

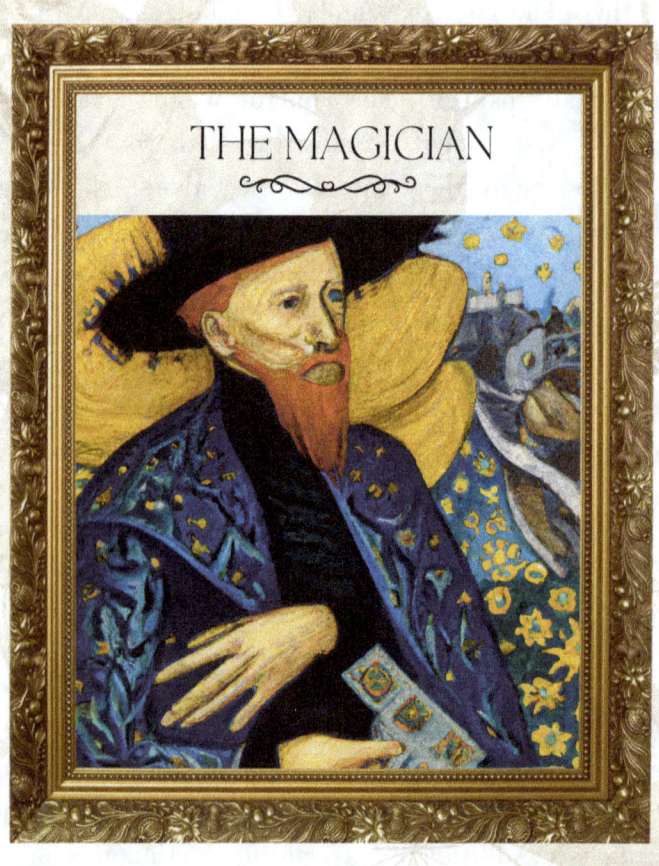

THE MAGICIAN

The card the guides have chosen for you is...

The Magician represents creativity, manifestation, and personal power. It symbolizes the ability to turn your ideas into reality and to bring your desires into being through the use of your own skills and abilities. The Magician represents a time of taking action, of making things happen, and of taking control of your life. It may also indicate that you have all the tools and resources you need to achieve your goals, and that you are capable of making things happen. The Magician can also suggest that it's a time for using your creativity and personal power to manifest your desires and to bring your dreams to life. However, The Magician also warns against using your power for selfish or unethical purposes. The Magician is a reminder to use your skills and abilities for good, to focus on your goals, and to make things happen with integrity and purpose.

Interpretation and Mantra...

You are actively working towards materializing your aspirations, and you possess the means to generate what you crave. You merge enchantment and pragmatism to transform your visions into tangible results.

Mantra "I harness my personal power, manifest my desires, and create my reality with integrity."

The card the guides have chosen for you is...

The Nine of Wands represents resilience, determination, and the ability to overcome obstacles. It can indicate that the individual is nearing the end of a difficult challenge and that they have the strength and willpower to see it through to the end. The image on often depicts a wounded warrior, leaning on a staff, and looking out over a battlefield. This imagery suggests that the individual has been through a lot and has had to fight hard to get to where they are, but they are not done yet. The Nine of Wands can also indicate that the individual has a strong sense of self-defense and is prepared to defend themselves if necessary. It can also be a reminder to be vigilant and to keep one's guard up, as there may be one last obstacle to overcome before achieving success.

Interpretation and Mantra...

Despite encountering hardship and weariness, you remain upright and unyielding. Your resilience, persistence, and willingness to do whatever it takes to reach your objective is remarkable. Keep persevering as you are very close to your goal. Don't allow others to discourage you.

Mantra: "Daily I develop my inner strength."

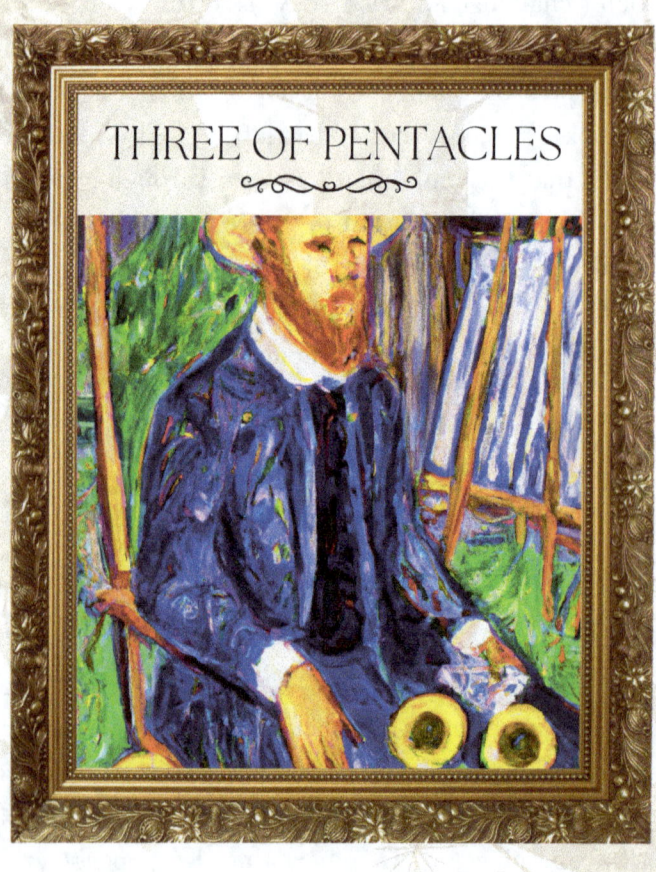

THREE OF PENTACLES

The card the guides have chosen for you is...

The Three of Pentacles tarot represents teamwork, collaboration, and creativity. It symbolizes a time of working together towards a common goal, often reflecting a sense of cooperation and collaboration. The image often depicts a master craftsman collaborating with his apprentices, symbolizing the sharing of skills and knowledge to achieve a common goal. The Three of Pentacles represents a desire to work together and a willingness to pool resources and skills towards a shared vision. This can indicate a time of creative collaboration, where one is working towards a common goal with others, leveraging the strengths of each person to achieve a greater outcome. It can also suggest a need to balance individual ambition with a focus on teamwork and collaboration. The Three of Pentacles tarot is a powerful symbol of teamwork, collaboration, and creativity.

Interpretation and Mantra...

You work collaboratively with others, seeking to create synergies and achieve significant results. You strike a balance between the experience and expertise of veterans, as well as the fresh ideas and perspectives of newcomers.

Mantra "*I work in partnership with others, collaborating towards a common goal. I balance my individual ambition with a focus on teamwork and collaboration.*

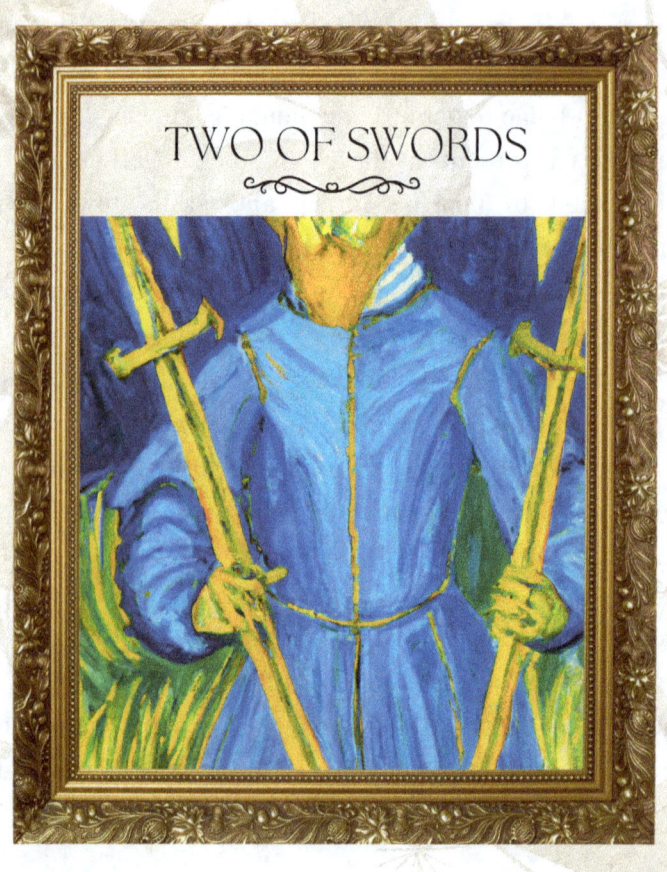

The card the guides have chosen for you is...

The Two of Swords in a tarot reading represents a state of indecision and being stuck between two options. This card can indicate that the querent is facing a difficult choice and that they are struggling to make a decision. It suggests a feeling of being torn between two paths or two different ideas. The Two of Swords also represents the need to find balance and to make a decision that is fair to all parties involved. It can indicate that the querent will have to weigh the pros and cons of each option and to make a decision that is in line with their values and beliefs. In a negative context, it may indicate that the querent is avoiding making a decision or that they are in denial about a certain situation. Overall, the Two of Swords is a reminder to find balance and to make a decision that is in line with your values and beliefs.

Interpretation and Mantra...

You are confronted with a difficult decision - at a crossroads - and uncertain about which direction to take. Take a closer look: there may be factors that are not immediately apparent that can assist you in making the correct choice.

Mantra "I find balance, weigh my options and make a decision that aligns with my values and beliefs."

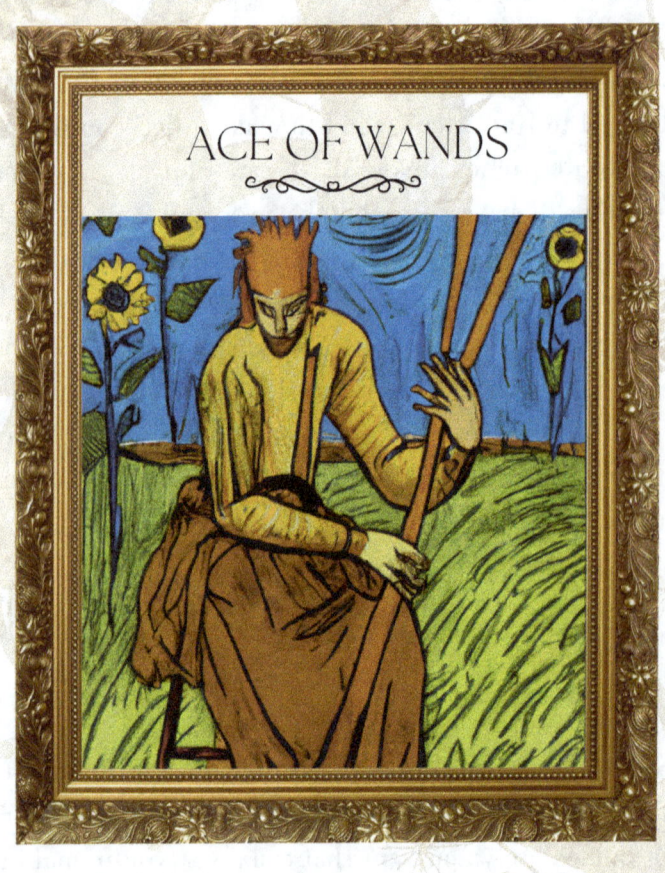

The card the guides have chosen for you is...

The Ace of Wands is from the Major Arcana in a tarot deck. It typically represents new beginnings, inspiration, creativity, and passion. It can also symbolize a new venture or opportunity, as well as a burst of energy and enthusiasm. The Ace of Wands can indicate that a new idea or project is on the horizon, and that now is the time to take action and pursue it. It can also suggest that a person is feeling confident and self-assured, and that they are ready to tackle new challenges and make things happen. In a reading, the Ace of Wands can be a sign of good luck and positive change, and it encourages the person to have faith in their abilities and to move forward with their plans.

Interpretation and Mantra...

You are brimming with motivation, energy, and novel ideas that spur growth. A world of potentiality is unfolding before you. Pursue your passion.

Mantra "I am filled with inspiration and creativity. I trust in my abilities and take bold action towards my goals. I am open to new opportunities and possibilities, and I embrace change with enthusiasm and energy."

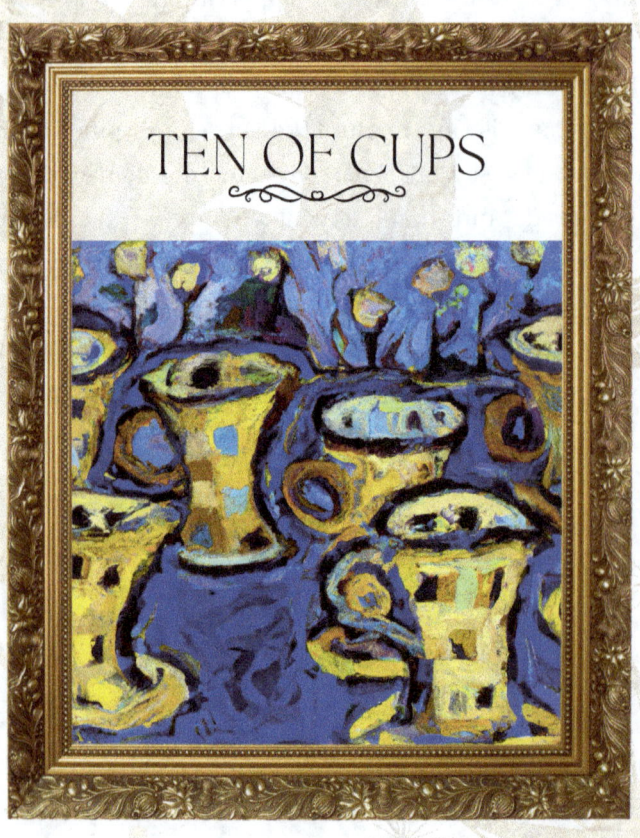

TEN OF CUPS

The card the guides have chosen for you is...

The Ten of Cups is uplifting and positive which symbolizes joy, harmony, and contentment. It suggests that your emotional and spiritual needs are being met and that you are feeling fulfilled in life. It can also be interpreted as a reminder to be thankful for all the blessings that you have. Ten of Cups can indicate that you have a strong, supportive family or community in your life. It can also suggest that you have achieved your goals and are now enjoying the rewards. The Ten of Cups can also be a sign that you are in a place of emotional and spiritual balance and that you have a strong sense of self-love and appreciation. The Ten of Cups is a reminder to savor the moments of joy and contentment in life, and to be grateful for all the blessings that you have.

Interpretation and Mantra...

By adhering to your heart and having faith in your intuition, you have fashioned a life filled with happiness and interconnectedness. Your associations with others feel whole, fulfilling, and in sync with your true self.

Mantra: "I am blessed with an abundance of love and joy in my life. I am grateful for the blessings that come my way."

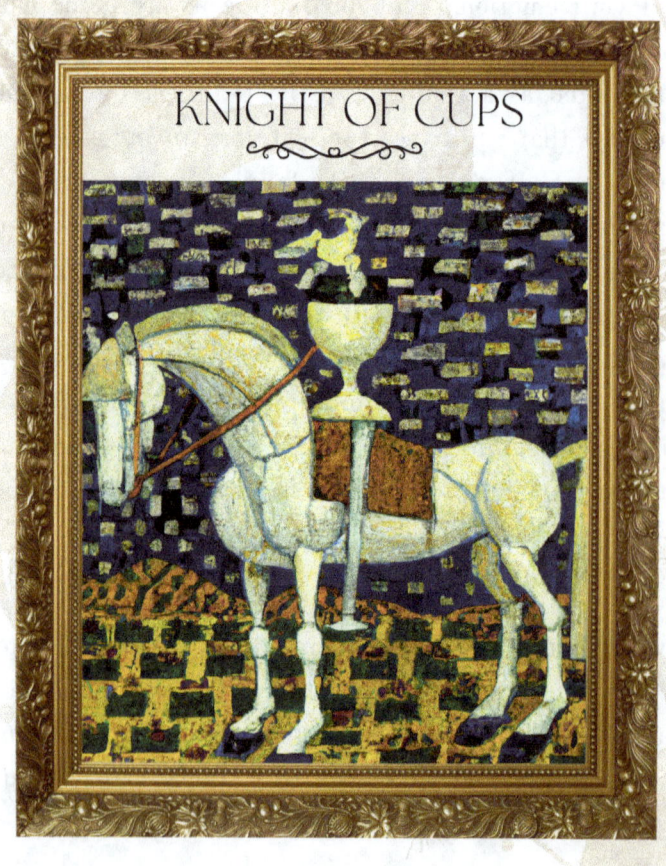

The card the guides have chosen for you is...

The Tarot Knight of Cups represents emotional sensitivity, creativity, and intuition. This card is associated with the water element, which represents emotions and feelings. The Knight of Cups symbolizes a deep connection with your emotions, a strong imagination, and a willingness to take risks in order to follow your heart. It may also represent a romantic interest, who is imaginative and intuitive, and who is able to bring excitement and passion into your life. However, the Knight of Cups can also indicate a tendency to get carried away by emotions and to make impulsive decisions without considering the consequences. Knight of Cups is a reminder to balance your emotional and intuitive nature with practicality and logic. The Knight of Cups suggests that it's a time for following your dreams and letting your heart guide you, but also to be mindful of the impact of your actions.

Interpretation and Mantra...

You possess a romantic and charismatic nature, and you have a fondness for the concept of love. You express your emotions openly and honestly. You flourish in the presence of beauty and find inspiration in various forms of artistic expression.

Mantra "*I listen to my heart and follow my passions. I balance my emotions with practicality and wisdom.*"

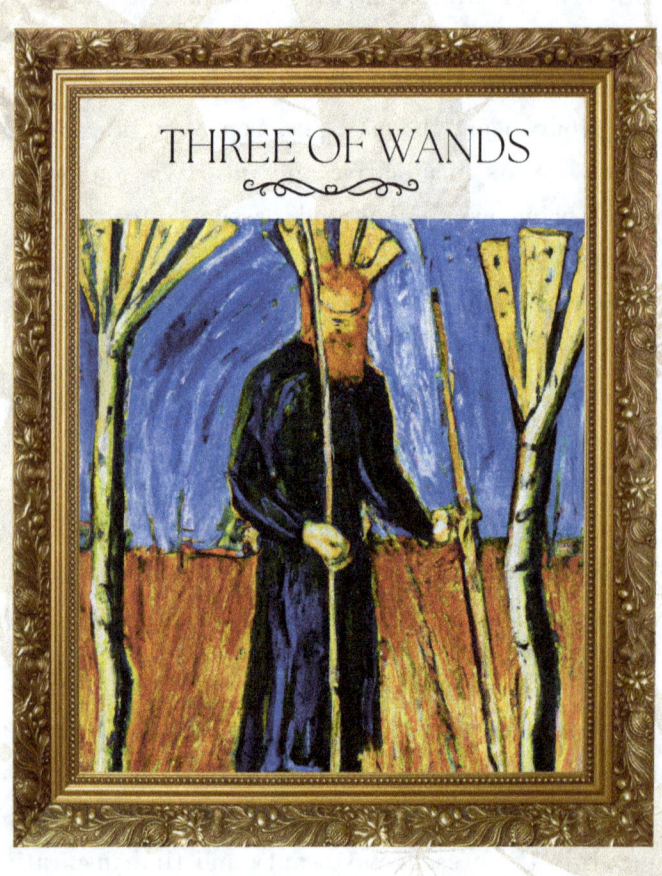

The card the guides have chosen for you is...

The Three of Wands tarot represents growth, expansion, and ambition. It symbolizes the beginning of a new venture or project and the potential for success in the future. It often signifies taking a risk and exploring new possibilities, with the figure on the card looking out over the horizon, eager to see what the future holds. The Three of Wands also represents a time of preparation, planning and building the foundation for future growth. This can indicate that one is at the brink of a major breakthrough and success is within reach. However, it may also indicate a need for caution, as new opportunities and challenges can bring unexpected twists and turns.

Interpretation and Mantra...

Step outside your comfort zone and venture into uncharted territory to seek new opportunities for growth and development. Explore new areas and broaden your horizons.

Mantra "I embrace growth, expansion and new opportunities. I trust in my vision and am confident in my ability to turn my plans into reality. I am ready to take bold actions and make my dreams a reality."

The card the guides have chosen for you is...

The Seven of Swords tarot represents a time of deception, cunning, and strategy. It symbolizes a time of feeling vulnerable and unsure, often reflecting a need to be cautious and protect oneself. The image often depicts a person sneaking away with seven swords, symbolizing a desire to act in one's own self-interest and be deceptive. The Seven of Swords represents a need to be strategic and protect oneself, leveraging cunning and cleverness to navigate through challenging situations. This can indicate a time of feeling vulnerable and unsure, where one must be cautious and protect themselves from being taken advantage of. It can also suggest a need to balance a focus on self-interest with a sense of honesty and integrity. The Seven of Swords tarot is a powerful symbol of deception, cunning, and strategy.

Interpretation and Mantra...

It is not feasible to tackle everything simultaneously. It is necessary to prioritize what matters most to you, even if it may disappoint others. There may be times when prioritizing your own needs is crucial to achieving what you desire.

Mantra "I protect myself with cunning and strategy. I am cautious and aware, always seeking to navigate through challenges. I balance my self-interest with honesty and integrity, always striving to do what is right."

PAGE OF SWORDS

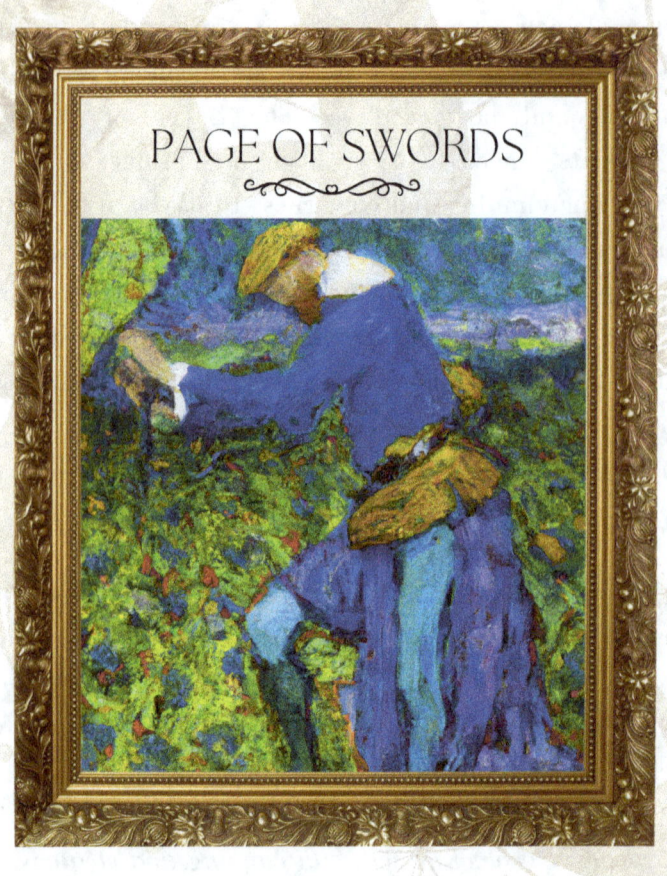

The card the guides have chosen for you is...

The Page of Swords tarot represents a time of communication, intelligence, and adaptability. It symbolizes a time of being curious and eager, often reflecting a desire to learn and explore new ideas. The image often depicts a young person holding a sword, symbolizing a sharp mind and a willingness to communicate and explore. The Page of Swords represents a desire to communicate and learn, leveraging your intelligence and adaptability to explore new ideas and perspectives. This can indicate a time of eagerness and curiosity, where one is open to new experiences and willing to take risks. It can also suggest a need to balance a focus on communication with a sense of compassion and empathy. The Page of Swords tarot is a powerful symbol of intelligence, communication, and adaptability.

Interpretation and Mantra...

Your inquisitive nature drives you to ask questions and seek out knowledge in various domains. As a natural communicator, you possess the ability to effectively share your message with others. You are now prepared to take the next step and share your message with the world.

Mantra "*I communicate with intelligence and adaptability. I am eager and curious, always seeking to learn and explore new ideas.*"

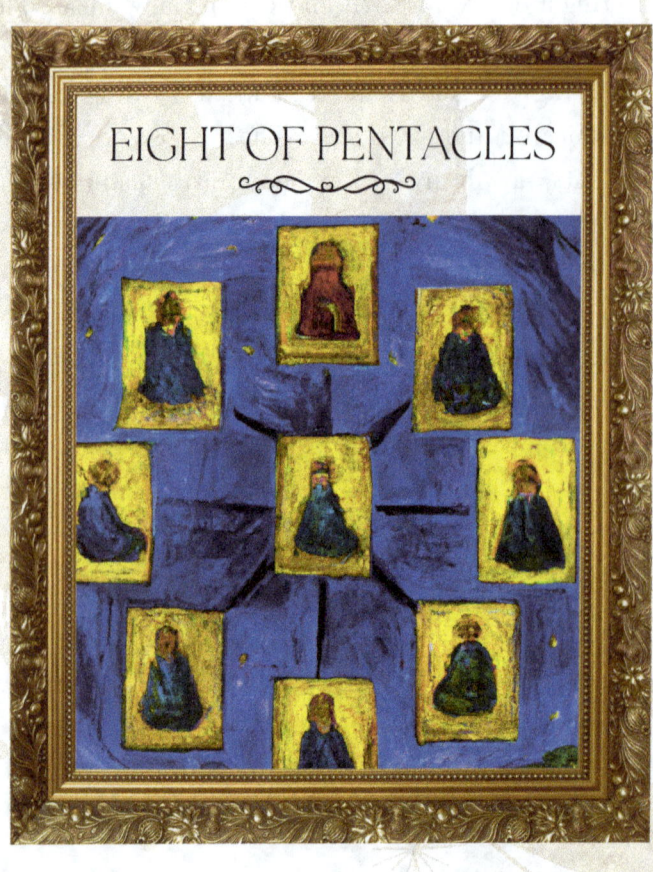

The card the guides have chosen for you is...

The Eight of Pentacles tarot represents hard work, dedication, and mastery. It symbolizes a time of honing one's skills and mastering a particular craft or trade. The image often depicts a craftsman working diligently at his workbench, symbolizing the focus and determination required to achieve mastery. The Eight of Pentacles represents a drive to succeed and a willingness to put in the effort required to reach one's goals. This can indicate a time of focused effort, where one is dedicated to improving their skills and knowledge. It can also suggest a need to balance one's focus on work with other important aspects of life, such as relationships and personal well-being. The Eight of Pentacles tarot is a powerful symbol of hard work, dedication, and mastery

Interpretation and Mantra...

By utilizing your determination, conscientiousness, and keen attention to detail, you are able to effectively accomplish tasks. With each repetition of the task, you gradually progress towards mastering your craft.

Mantra   *"I am dedicated to mastering my craft and achieving my goals. I work hard and put in the effort required to reach success."*

THE STAR

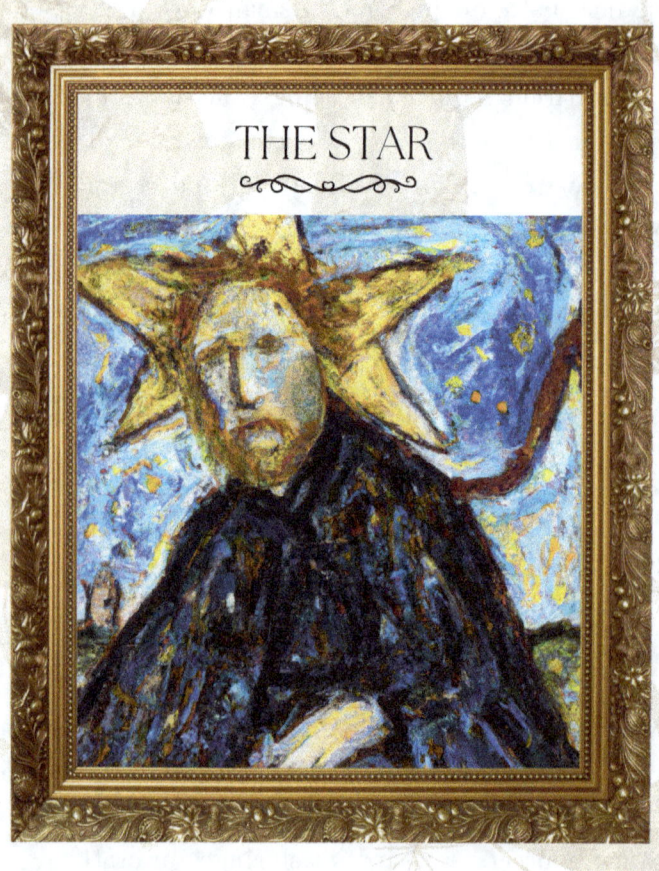

The card the guides have chosen for you is...

The Star tarot represents hope, inspiration, and renewal. It symbolizes a time of healing and self-discovery, often reflecting a need to find a sense of peace and balance. The image often depicts a naked figure reaching towards a shining star, symbolizing a desire to connect with one's inner wisdom and find hope in difficult times. The Star represents a need to find hope and inspiration, leveraging a sense of peace and balance to heal and renew. This can indicate a time of self-discovery and inner growth, where one must look within to find their own truth and purpose. It can also suggest a need to balance a focus on the future with a sense of gratitude for the present moment. The Star tarot is a powerful symbol of hope, inspiration, and renewal.

Interpretation and Mantra...

You are currently in a potent phase of creative energy, which can be channeled through your genuine self. It is vital to remain receptive to new possibilities while staying true to your authentic self. By having faith and trust in the Universe, you can tap into its gifts and blessings, which are waiting to be shared with you.

Mantra "I find hope and inspiration within. I am at peace, always seeking to balance my mind and body. I connect with my inner wisdom, always striving to discover my own truth and purpose."

The card the guides have chosen for you is...

The Tarot Six of Swords represents a journey, transition, and movement towards a more positive future. It is associated with the air element, which represents communication, movement, and change. The Six of Swords symbolizes a time of transition, moving from a difficult or challenging situation towards a more positive future. This may indicate that you are leaving behind a difficult situation, making a change, or moving on to a better future. The Six of Swords can also suggest that you are seeking clarity and understanding, and that you are looking for a way to move forward. This card is a reminder to trust in the journey, to be open to change and new opportunities, and to have faith in a brighter future. The Six of Swords suggests that it's a time for making changes, for letting go of the past, and for moving towards a more positive future.

Interpretation and Mantra...

You find yourself in a transitional phase - a relocation, a ceremonial milestone, or a mental transformation of sorts. You are departing from what was familiar and comfortable, in pursuit of the unfamiliar. This change is crucial for your personal development.

Mantra "I navigate through change with grace and release my emotional burdens."

The card the guides have chosen for you is...

The Page of Cups tarot represents emotion, intuition, and creativity. It can indicate that the querent is in a time of emotional awakening and that they are being called to tap into their intuition and creativity. It suggests a feeling of emotional sensitivity and a strong connection to one's feelings. The Page of Cups also represents the ability to trust your instincts and to listen to your heart. It can indicate that the querent will have to follow their intuition and to trust their emotions in order to move forward. In a negative context, it may indicate that the querent is too emotional and not being logical or objective. Overall, the Page of Cups is a reminder to trust your emotions, tap into your intuition and to let your creativity flow.

Interpretation and Mantra...

An unexpected opportunity or creative idea has presented itself to you, bringing with it a sense of excitement and possibility. You may be filled with optimistic thoughts about the potential outcomes. Keep an open mind and be prepared for pleasant surprises.

Mantra "*I trust my emotions, tap into my intuition and let my creativity flow, following my heart's guidance.*"

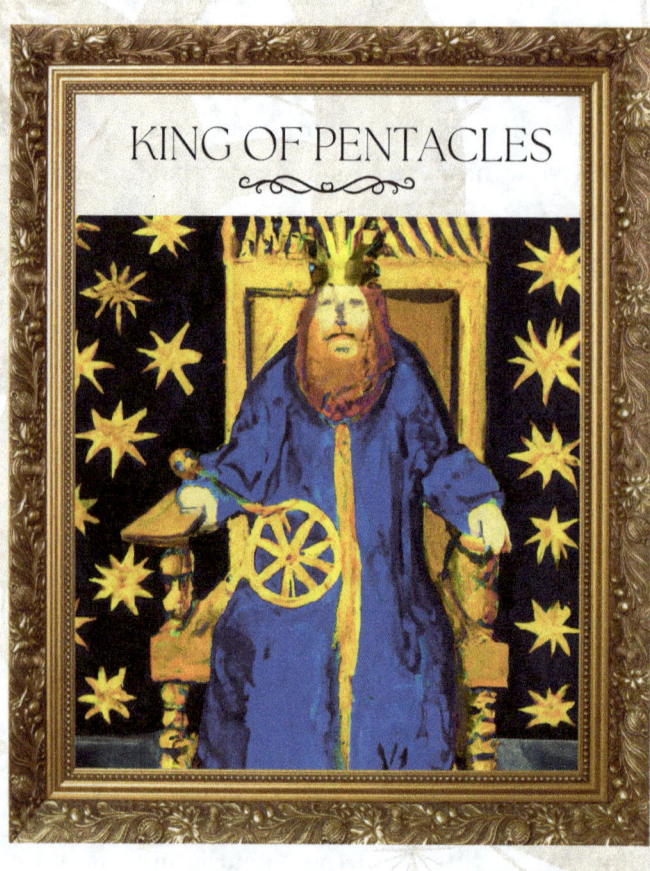

The card the guides have chosen for you is...

The King of Pentacles is a tarot that represents stability, security and material wealth. He is a powerful and practical figure who is able to manifest his desires into reality through hard work and determination. This can indicate that a person is in a position of power and control in their financial or professional life, and that they have the resources and ability to make things happen. The King of Pentacles can also suggest that a person is feeling secure and content in their material possessions and is able to enjoy the fruits of their labor. It can also indicate that a person is very reliable and dependable, and is a good provider for their family and loved ones. Overall, the King of Pentacles is a positive tarot that suggests success and abundance in the material realm.

Interpretation and Mantra...

You are confident, attracting and managing wealth. You can translate yor vision into something that is tangible, practical, and often lucrative. You are the ultimate business owner.

Mantra "I manifest abundance and prosperity in my life through hard work and determination."

THREE OF SWORDS

The card the guides have chosen for you is...

The Three of Swords in a tarot reading represents heartbreak, emotional pain, and betrayal. This card can indicate that the querent is experiencing a time of emotional turmoil and that they are going through a difficult break-up or a betrayal by someone they trust. It suggests a feeling of being stabbed in the back and a sense of loss. The Three of Swords also represents the ability to overcome emotional pain and to move on from a difficult situation. It can indicate that the querent will have to face their pain and to let go of something or someone that is causing them suffering. In a negative context, it may indicate that the querent is holding on to pain and is unable to move on. Overall, the Three of Swords is a reminder to process and release emotional pain, and to learn from difficult experiences.

Interpretation and Mantra...

You are experiencing hurt and disappointment, internalizing the negative words of others. You are beset by emotions of loss, heartbreak, grief, and sorrow. Remember that these feelings are transitory. Focus on releasing the pain and granting forgiveness to those who have caused you hurt.

Mantra "I acknowledge and release emotional pain, learning from difficult experiences and moving forward with strength and resilience."

WHEEL OF FORTUNE

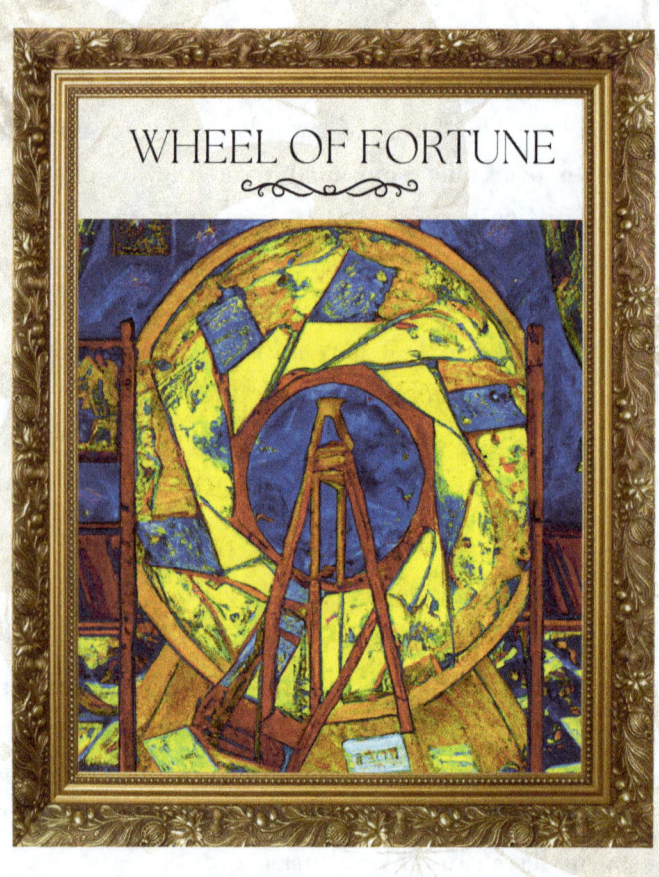

The card the guides have chosen for you is...

The Tarot the Wheel of Fortune represents the cyclical nature of life and the inevitability of change. The wheel symbolizes the ups and downs of life and the concept that what goes around comes around. This suggests that events, circumstances, and fortune are beyond our control and are subject to a greater cosmic force. It may indicate a turning point in one's life, either for better or for worse. It can also suggest a sense of destiny or fate and the idea that we are all part of a larger pattern. The Wheel of Fortune can be seen as both positive and negative, reminding us to be prepared for both good and bad experiences and to embrace change as a natural part of life.

Interpretation and Mantra...

You are going through the natural cycle of change. The wheel is in motion, and your circumstances are constantly transforming and shifting. As the saying goes, what goes up must come down, and the opposite is also true.

Mantra "I embrace change and trust in the journey of life."

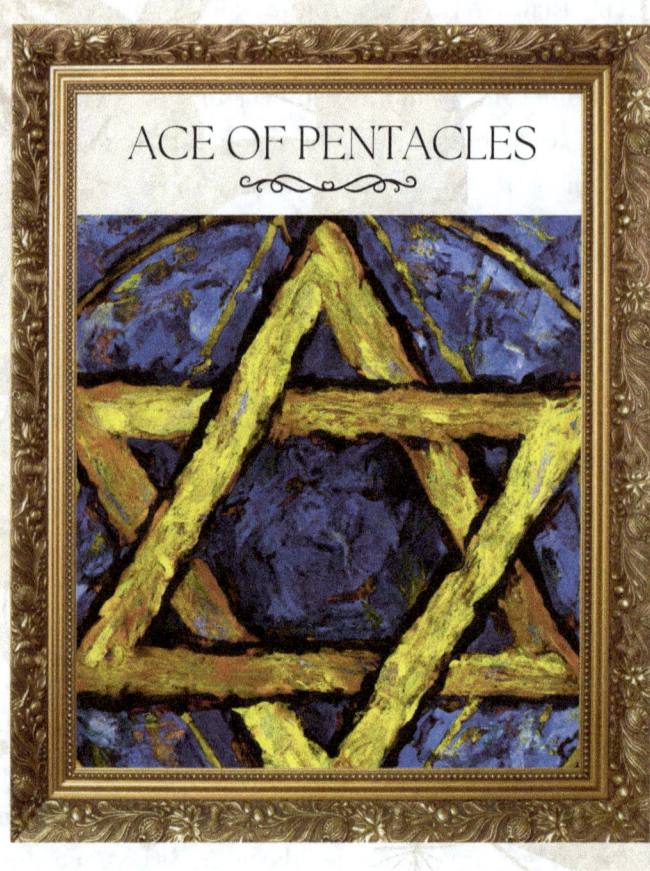

ACE OF PENTACLES

The card the guides have chosen for you is...

The Ace of Pentacles represents new beginnings and opportunities in the areas of wealth, stability, and prosperity. The Ace of Pentacles symbolizes a fresh start and the possibility of material abundance, and can indicate the arrival of a new job, a business venture, or a financial windfall. When the Ace of Pentacles appears in a reading, it encourages you to embrace new opportunities, to focus on building a strong foundation, and to put your trust in the universe to bring you what you need. Whether you are starting a new business, seeking a new job, or simply seeking to improve your financial situation, the Ace of Pentacles can serve as a powerful reminder that abundance is available to you, and that you are capable of attracting it into your life. By focusing on your goals, taking practical steps to achieve them, and trusting in the universe to support you, you can bring abundance and stability into your life

Interpretation and Mantra...

You have a new prospect before you that holds promise of growing into a lucrative and prosperous venture. This opportunity could be a business idea, job offer, or financial investment. It's important to manifest your aspirations in a concrete and practical manner, making them tangible and achievable.

Mantra "I trust in the universe to bring me abundance and stability."

THE HANGED MAN

The card the guides have chosen for you is...

The Hanged Man represents sacrifice, surrender, and letting go. It can indicate that the querent is in a state of suspension and that they are at a turning point in their life, where they are being called to let go of something. It suggests a feeling of being stuck and not knowing which way to go. The Hanged Man also represents the ability to look at things from a different perspective and to gain a new understanding. It can indicate that the querent will have to let go of something to gain a new understanding, a new way of seeing things or a new outcome. In a negative context, it may indicate that the querent is being too passive and not taking action to change their situation. Overall, the Hanged Man is a reminder to let go of what's no longer serving you, to gain a new perspective and to take a new path.

Interpretation and Mantra...

You are currently in a state of limbo and awaiting guidance or new information. Take a step back and try to see your situation from a different angle to gain new insights and clarity.

Mantra "*I let go of what no longer serves me, gaining new perspective and embracing change as I step into a new path.*"

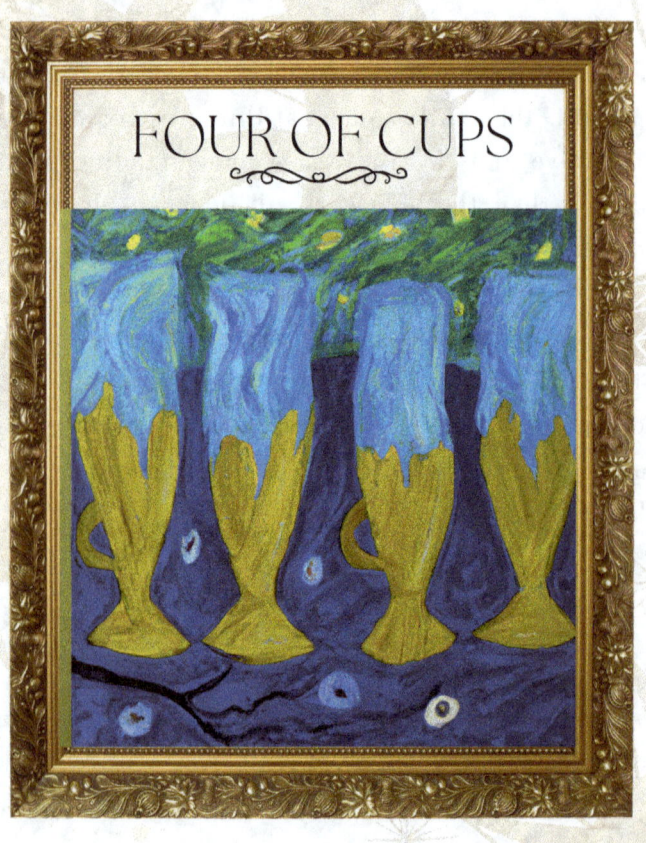

The card the guides have chosen for you is…

The Four of Cups in a tarot reading represents contemplation, introspection, and dissatisfaction. It often appears when a person is feeling unfulfilled or unappreciative of what they have. The figure is often depicted sitting under a tree with three cups in front of them, and a fourth cup being offered by a hand from above, representing the potential for something more. The Four of Cups can indicate that a person is feeling ungrateful for what they have and may be missing out on something greater.

It can also indicate that a person may be feeling bored or stuck in their current situation, and that they are in need of change. It can represent a feeling of dissatisfaction and a longing for something more. The Four of Cups can also indicate a need to take time for self-reflection and introspection, to evaluate what one truly wants and needs in life. It can indicate a need to reassess one's goals and to make changes in order to move forward.

Interpretation and Mantra…

Despite offers and opportunities coming your way, you are currently declining them. Take time to reflect on your subsequent move and concentrate on what matters most to you.

Mantra: I am grateful for all the love around me for me, even if I am unable to feel it.

The card the guides have chosen for you is...

The Ace of Cups tarot symbolizes the beginning of a new emotional journey and represents the start of a new era of love, happiness, and fulfillment. The image often depicts a hand emerging from the clouds holding a cup, symbolizing the abundance of emotions and love that is being offered. The Ace of Cups tarot is a powerful symbol of new beginnings and the potential for emotional growth and fulfillment. It suggests a time of opening up to new experiences and embracing the flow of emotions, whether it be romantic love, self-love, or the love of others. This can indicate a time of happiness and joy, where one is able to connect with their feelings and find fulfillment in their relationships and life. Whether you are looking to start a new relationship, deepen existing ones, or simply find more happiness in your life, the Ace of Cups is a powerful reminder of the potential for emotional growth and fulfillment.

Interpretation and Mantra...

You are brimming with delight, elation, and ecstasy. A plethora of creative possibilities await you. There is a chance for fresh romances, friendships, or artistic endeavors to come your way.

Mantra "I open my heart to love, joy, and fulfillment."

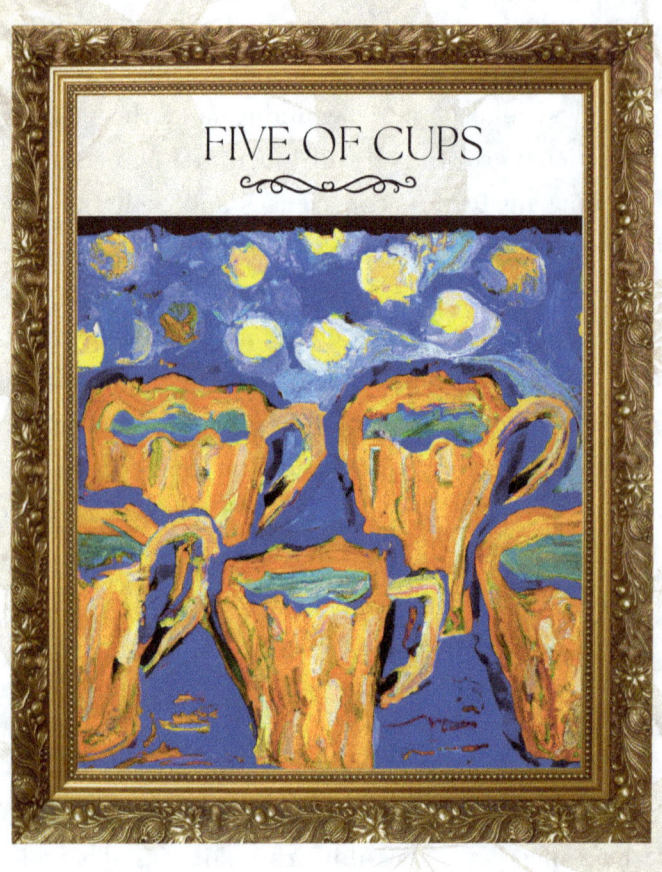

The card the guides have chosen for you is...

The Five of Cups represents disappointment, loss, and grief. It is associated with the astrological sign of Scorpio, which is known for its intense emotions and transformative nature. The imagery often depicts a person standing before three spilled cups with two more standing behind them, symbolizing the loss of something important. The Five of Cups can indicate that the querent is feeling a sense of loss or disappointment, and they may be dwelling on past regrets or mistakes. It can also suggest that the querent is experiencing emotional turmoil and may be feeling overwhelmed by their feelings.

However, the Five of Cups is not all negative, as it also carries a message of understanding that sometimes, we must lose something to gain something else.

Interpretation and Mantra...

A situation has not transpired as you envisioned, leaving you feeling despondent, remorseful, and let down. However, before you become entirely immersed in your melancholy, take a moment to survey your surroundings. There are numerous fresh opportunities awaiting you when you are prepared for them.

Mantra "I honour my grief and loss, I release the past and embrace the future. I trust in the healing power of time."

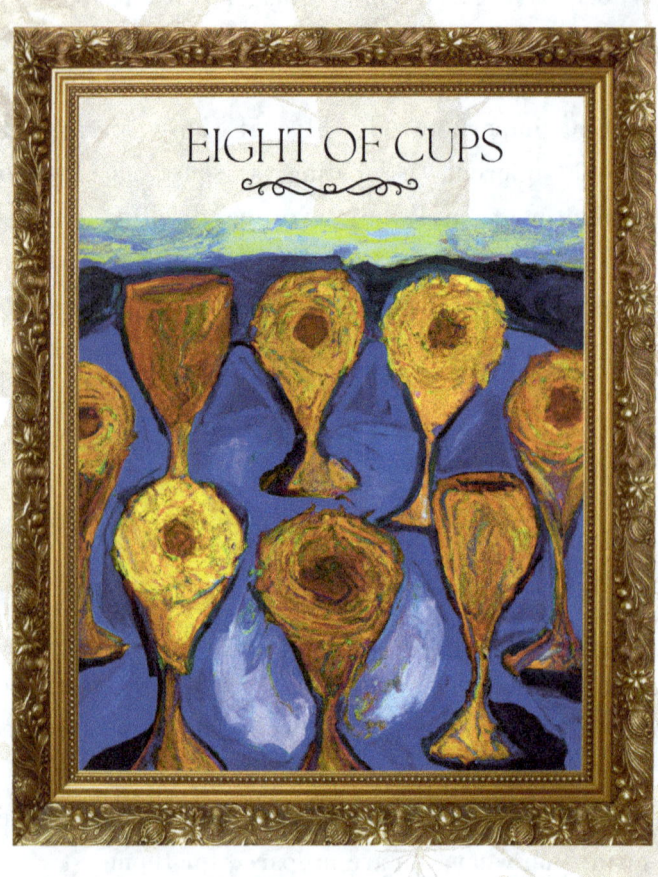

The card the guides have chosen for you is...

The Tarot Eight of Cups is often associated with emotional and spiritual dissatisfaction, as well as a sense of emptiness. This can indicate that the querent is feeling unfulfilled in their current situation and is ready to move on to something new. The image on the often depicts a figure walking away from eight cups that are arranged in a symmetrical pattern. The cups symbolize the querent's past experiences and emotions, and the figure's decision to leave them behind represents their desire to move forward and find something more fulfilling. The Eight of Cups can also represent a time of introspection and self-discovery, as the querent seeks to understand their own needs and desires. Ultimately, the Eight of Cups encourages the querent to take a risk and pursue what brings them true happiness and fulfillment.

Interpretation and Mantra...

It is time to let go of a disappointing situation or relationship. While you may have hoped it would work out, it is clear that it is not meant to be. It is best to move forward and focus on the opportunities ahead.

Mantra "I embrace change and follow my heart."

KING OF SWORDS

The card the guides have chosen for you is...

The King of Swords in a tarot reading represents a figure of authority and leadership, characterized by logic, rationality, and mental acuity. This card can indicate that the querent is in a position of power or authority, and it suggests a clear and decisive mind. The King of Swords also represents the ability to make difficult decisions and to see things objectively. It can indicate that the querent will have to make a difficult decision or that they will have to rely on their intellect and ability to think critically. In a negative context, it may indicate a lack of empathy and an over-reliance on logic to the detriment of emotions. Overall, the King of Swords is a reminder to use your intellect and critical thinking skills to make sound decisions and to lead with integrity and fairness.

Interpretation and Mantra...

You are in command, leading from a position of authority. You employ your analytical capabilities and intellect to evaluate the present circumstance and reach well-informed conclusions based on your discernment of the truth.

Mantra "I use my intellect and reason to make fair and just decisions, leading with integrity and objectivity."

The card the guides have chosen for you is...

The Judgement represents a time of self-reflection and self-evaluation, a time of judgement and decision making. Judgement can indicate that the querent is being called to a higher purpose, and it suggests a feeling of being judged or judged by others. The Judgement also represents the ability to forgive oneself and others, and to let go of past mistakes and regrets. It can indicate that the querent will have to make amends or to take responsibility for their actions. In a negative context, Judgement may indicate that the querent is being too hard on themselves or others and it can be a sign of being too judgemental. Overall, Judgement is a reminder to let go of past mistakes and to strive to be the best version of yourself, to be forgiving and to make amends when necessary.

Interpretation and Mantra...

This is your time to rise up! You are experiencing a huge spiritual awakening and realizing that you are destined for so much more. This is your cosmic uplevelling! Be ready to tune into a higher frequency.

Mantra "*I forgive myself and others, let go of past mistakes, and strive to be the best version of myself.*"

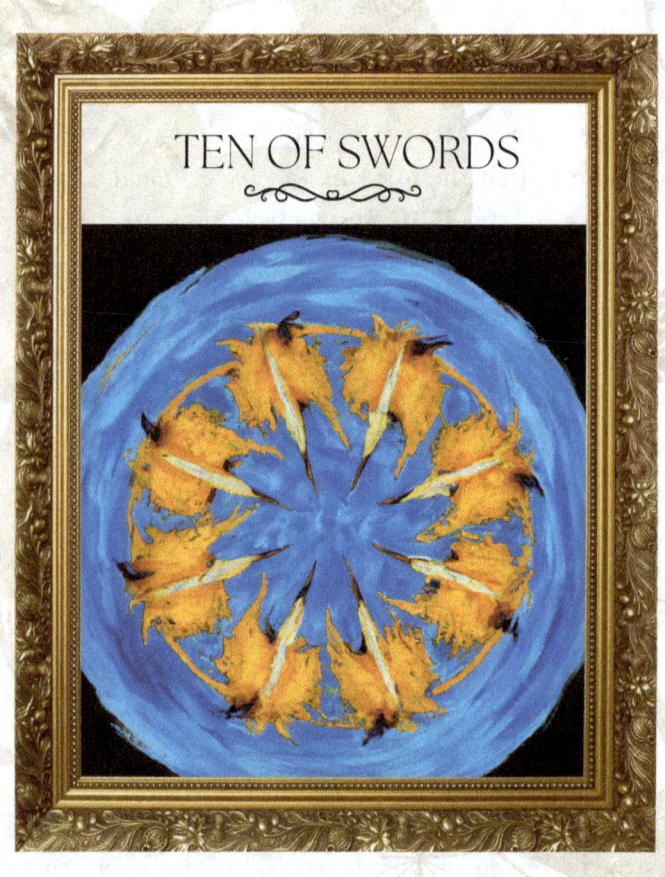

The card the guides have chosen for you is...

The Ten of Swords tarot represents a painful ending or betrayal. It symbolizes the experience of being stabbed in the back, either literally or figuratively. This can indicate a sudden, unexpected event that causes immense emotional pain and a feeling of being betrayed. It can also represent a deep loss or grief. The ten swords in the image symbolizes the final straw and the ultimate expression of suffering. The overall meaning of the Ten of Swords card suggests that you are currently experiencing a difficult ending or a loss that feels devastating. Ten of Swords asks you to face the pain and embrace the process of healing. It is important to remember that even though the situation may feel unbearable, there is a light at the end of the tunnel and growth will come from this experience. In life there is struggle, but if we did not struggle, we would not learn.

Interpretation and Mantra...

You are going through a sudden or traumatic conclusion that is causing significant distress. However, on a positive note, this ending is making room for new possibilities to arise.

Mantra "I honor my pain and embrace the journey of healing. I trust that this ending marks a new beginning and growth will come from this experience."

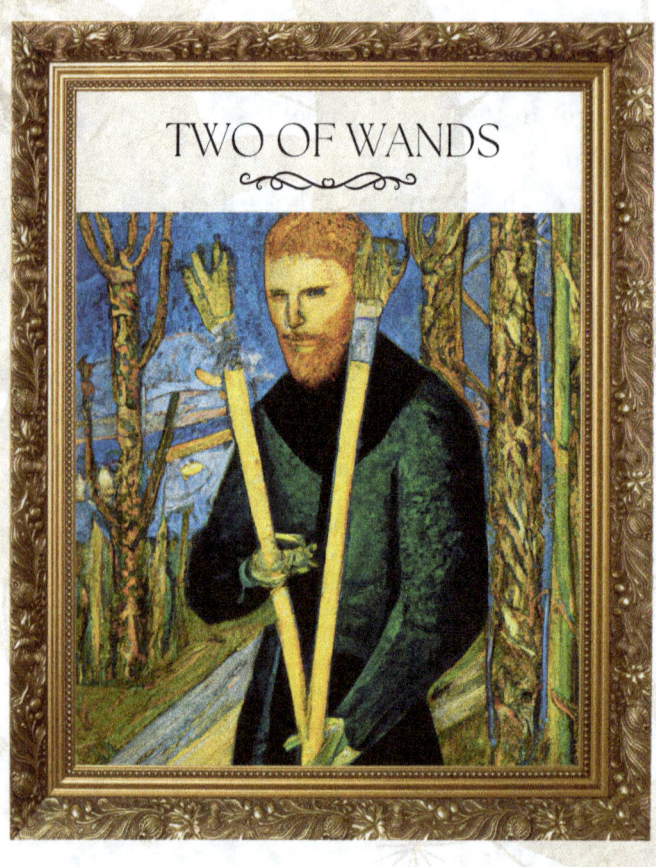

The card the guides have chosen for you is...

The tarot Two of Wands represents exploration, ambition, and vision. It symbolizes the beginning of a journey, whether it is a physical journey, an inner journey of self-discovery, or a journey towards realizing one's goals and aspirations. This card signifies that you are at the start of a new chapter in your life and that you have the courage and determination to make it a success. It is a call to action, urging you to step out of your comfort zone, take risks, and follow your intuition. The Two of Wands suggests that you have the potential to achieve great things, but it also warns that there may be obstacles and challenges along the way.

It invites you to think big, to set ambitious goals, and to pursue your dreams with passion and purpose. Whether you are seeking adventure, personal growth, or professional success, the Two of Wands is a positive omen, signaling that you have the power to make your dreams a reality.

Interpretation and Mantra...

You have a clear idea of what you want to manifest, and your focus now is to determine the path forward. You are actively exploring all possible options and meticulously planning ahead before taking action. Trust your intuition and let your passion drive you as you finalize your next steps.

Mantra   "*I trust my intuition, I am confident and brave, I seize opportunities and bring my vision to life.*"

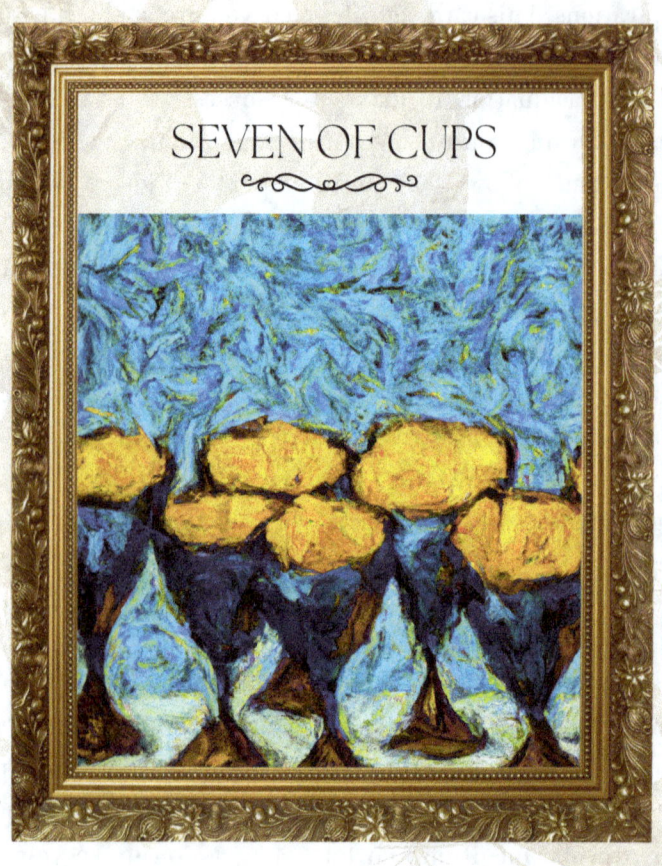

The card the guides have chosen for you is...

The Seven of Cups tarot represents a time of illusion and confusion. It symbolizes a period of indecision, where one is faced with multiple choices and paths. The image often depicts a figure surrounded by seven cups, each representing a different temptation or opportunity. The Seven of Cups represents a need to navigate through illusions and confusion, choosing the path that will bring the most fulfillment. This can indicate a time of self-discovery and inner growth, where one must look within to find their own truth and purpose. It can also suggest a need to balance a focus on the future with a sense of gratitude for the present moment. The Seven of Cups tarot is a powerful symbol of illusion, confusion, and indecision.

Interpretation and Mantra...

There are numerous options at your disposal that require your decision-making. However, it's crucial to exercise caution as you may be susceptible to delusions and impractical expectations. Assess your options thoroughly and delve deeper to unearth the true implications of each alternative.

Mantra "I navigate through illusions, embracing clarity and purpose. I choose wisely, always finding fulfillment in my path."

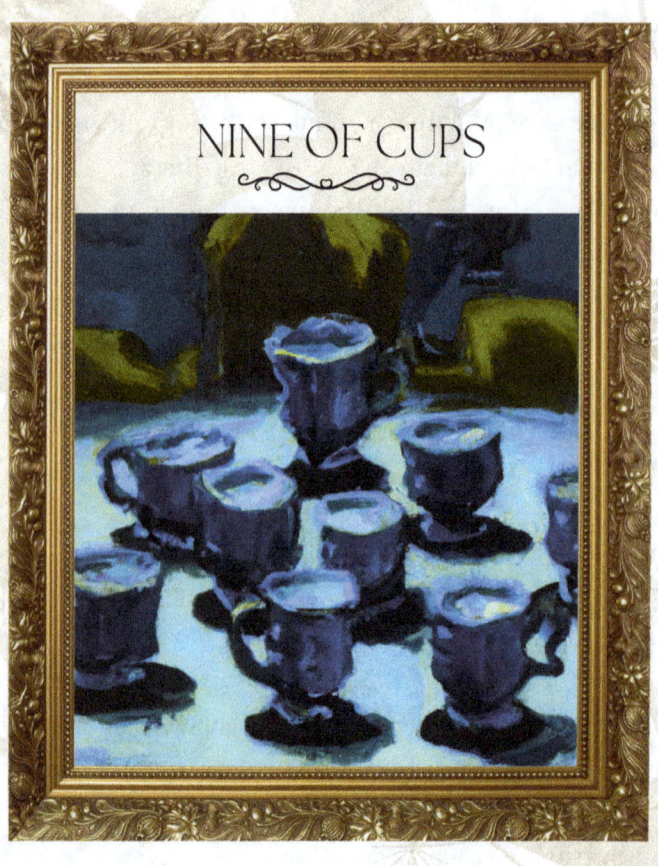

The card the guides have chosen for you is...

The Nine of Cups, is also known as "The Wish"," represents satisfaction, contentment, and happiness. It is associated with the water element, which represents emotions and feelings. The Nine of Cups symbolizes a time of feeling fulfilled, content, and satisfied with your life. Nine of Cups may indicate that your wishes and desires have been realized and that you are now experiencing a sense of happiness and contentment. The Nine of Cups can also suggest that it's a time for celebrating your achievements, for indulging in your pleasures, and for feeling grateful for all that you have. The Nine of Cups is a reminder to appreciate what you have, to enjoy the moment, and to bask in the warm glow of happiness and satisfaction. The Nine of Cups suggests that it's a time for celebrating your accomplishments, for feeling grateful for your blessings, and for embracing a sense of happiness and contentment in your life.

Interpretation and Mantra...

You feel a profound sense of contentment with your current circumstances. The celestial bodies seem to have synchronized, and you have obtained all that you desired. Take stock of your blessings and express appreciation for what you have brought into existence.

Mantra "I am grateful for my blessings, celebrate my achievements, and bask in the warm glow of happiness and contentment."

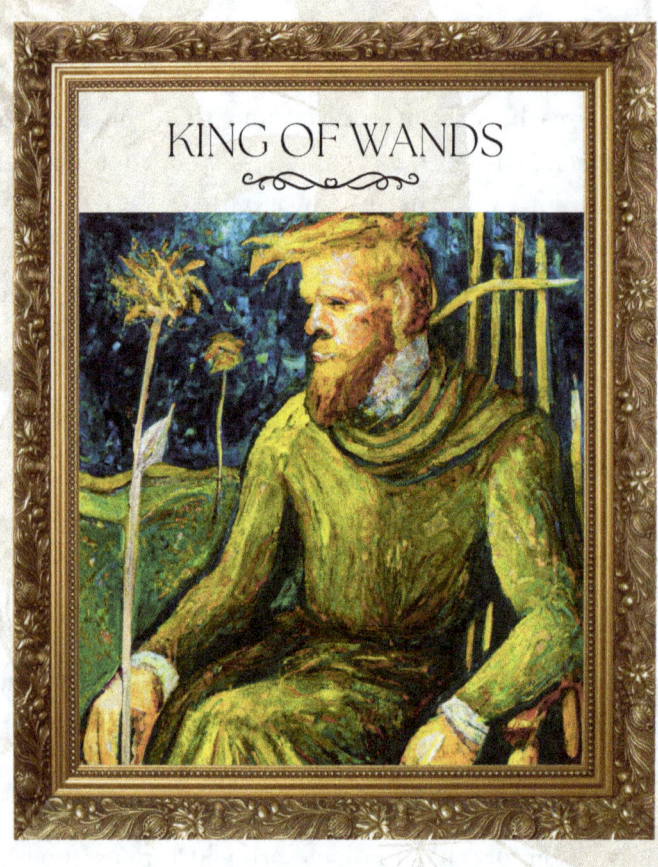

The card the guides have chosen for you is...

The King of Wands tarot represents a time of confidence, leadership, and passion. It symbolizes a period of courage and creativity, where one takes the initiative and makes things happen. The King of Wands represents a strong and dynamic energy, one that inspires and motivates others. The image often depicts a regal figure holding a wand, symbolizing the power and strength they bring to the table. The King of Wands tarot is a powerful symbol of leadership, courage, and creativity. It suggests a time of taking the initiative, pursuing your passions with confidence, and inspiring others with your vision and drive. This can indicate a time of growth and success, where one is able to make things happen and bring their ideas to life. Whether you are an entrepreneur, artist, or simply someone looking to make a positive impact, the King of Wands is a powerful reminder of your potential for success and achievement.

Interpretation and Mantra...

As a visionary leader, you are well-equipped to guide your team towards a shared objective. Your charisma, focus, and unwavering determination draw others towards you. You skillfully utilize social connections to achieve your goals.

Mantra "I am a leader, driven by passion and confidence. I inspire and motivate, bringing my vision to life."

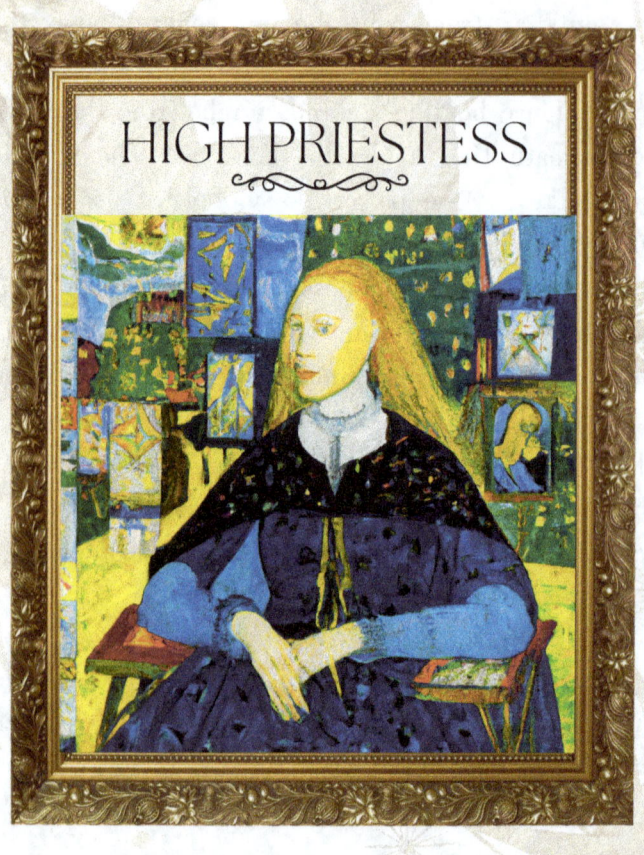

HIGH PRIESTESS

The card the guides have chosen for you is...

The High Priestess tarot represents intuition, secrets, and hidden knowledge. She is often depicted as a mysterious and enigmatic figure, representing the unconscious and the realm of the unknown. It suggests that the answers you seek are not easily accessible through logic and reason, but rather through your intuition and inner wisdom. It can indicate that you should trust your gut feelings and pay attention to your inner voice.

The High Priestess also represents a time of reflection and introspection. It can indicate that now is the time to withdraw and focus on your inner self, rather than external influences. The High Priestess can also indicate that there is something being kept secret or hidden and that you should be aware of this when making decisions.

In a relationship, it can indicate that trust and communication are key.

Interpretation and Mantra...

You are in sync with your intuition and your elevated self. The solutions you require are within you. Tap into your inner wisdom and embrace your divine feminine energy.

Mantra: "I trust my intuition and honor the wisdom within me. I am open to the mysteries of the universe and allow them to guide me on my path."

THE MOON

The card the guides have chosen for you is...

The Tarot The Moon represents the unconscious mind, emotions, and intuition. It is often associated with fear, uncertainty, and confusion, and can indicate a need to confront and understand one's deepest fears and anxieties. The image on the card typically features a full moon shining down on two towers and a path leading to a body of water, symbolizing the journey into the unknown and the exploration of the unconscious. This can suggest that there is something hidden or unknown that needs to be brought to light in order to move forward. It may also indicate a need to trust your instincts and emotions, and to allow your imagination and creativity to guide you. When The Moon appears in a reading, it can signal a time of confusion and uncertainty, but also of growth and self-discovery. It may indicate a need to look within, to listen to your inner voice, and to embrace the mystery and unpredictability of life.

Interpretation and Mantra...

Tap into your intuition and subconscious thoughts. You are attuned to the gentle rhythms of nature, particularly the phases of the moon. Permit yourself to be carried by these energies.

Mantra "I trust my instincts and surrender to the mystery."

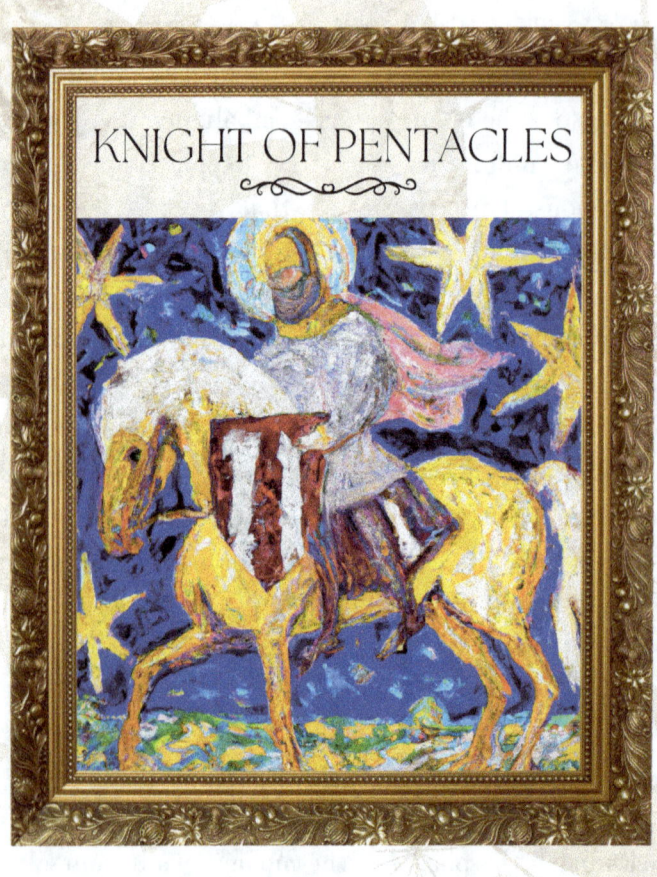

The card the guides have chosen for you is...

The Tarot Knight of Pentacles represents practicality, hard work, and persistence. It is associated with the earth element, which represents stability and material abundance. The Knight of Pentacles symbolizes a time of hard work, diligence, and persistence in pursuing your goals. The Knight of Pentacles may indicate that you are putting in the effort and taking the necessary steps to achieve your goals, and that you are making progress towards your desired outcome. The Knight of Pentacles can also suggest that it's a time for being practical, focused, and disciplined in your approach to work, finances, and other areas of your life. It is a reminder to be patient, persistent, and to stay focused on your long-term goals, even when faced with challenges or obstacles. The Knight of Pentacles suggests that it's a time for working hard, being disciplined, and making progress towards your desired outcomes.

Interpretation and Mantra...

You are diligent and responsible, adhering to the routines that have proven successful for you previously. You progress steadily towards your objectives, methodically completing your tasks. You have a talent for planning and executing plans seamlessly.

Mantra   "I work hard, stay focused, and persist in pursuing my goals."

The card the guides have chosen for you is...

The King of Cups is a tarot that represents emotional balance, wisdom, and diplomacy. It is associated with the element of water and is often seen as a symbol of calm and serenity. In a reading, the King of Cups may indicate that the querent is in a position of leadership and is able to handle emotional matters with grace and maturity. He may also represent a father figure, mentor or counselor who is kind, understanding and able to provide emotional support. The King of Cups also indicates that the querent has a strong connection to their intuition, and is able to navigate emotional situations with insight and empathy. In a negative context, the King of Cups can indicate emotional manipulation, being too passive or a lack of assertiveness.

Interpretation and Mantra...

You possess emotional regulation and the maturity to experience your feelings without permitting them to overpower you. You strike a harmonious balance between your intellect and emotions, and you are adept at managing both your internal and external environments.

Mantra "I am a leader in my emotions, understanding and guiding with compassion and empathy."

TWO OF PENTACLES

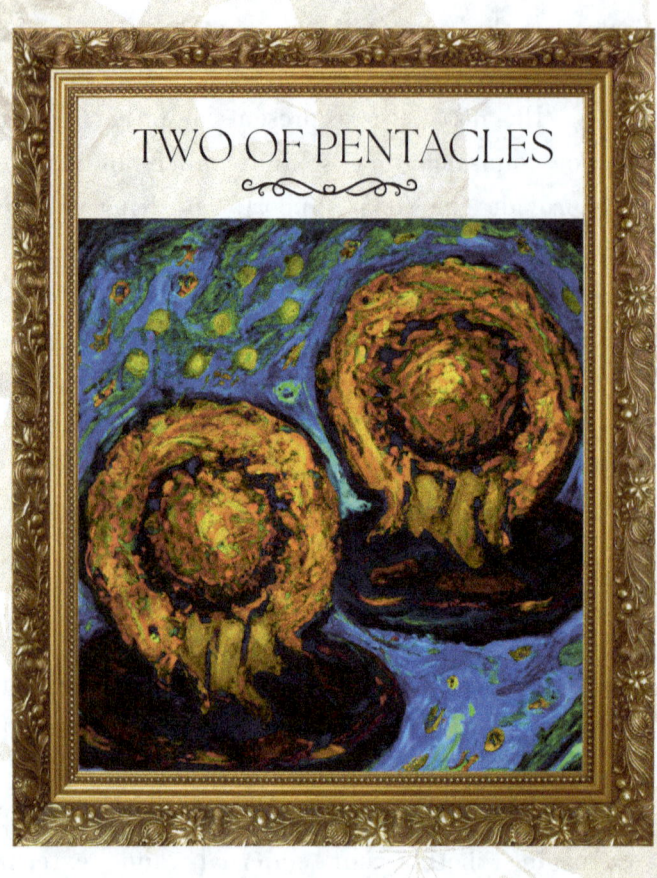

The card the guides have chosen for you is...

The Tarot card Two of Pentacles represents balance, versatility, and juggling multiple responsibilities. This card is associated with the earth element, which represents stability and material abundance. The Two of Pentacles symbolizes a time of juggling multiple responsibilities and maintaining balance in all areas of your life. This card may indicate that you are facing multiple demands on your time and energy, but that you are also capable of handling them all. The Two of Pentacles can also suggest that it's a time for finding balance in your finances, work, and relationships, and for making decisions that benefit both your short-term and long-term goals. This card is a reminder to be flexible, adaptable, and to have a sense of humor when faced with challenges. The Two of Pentacles suggests that it's a time for balancing your various responsibilities, for maintaining stability and focus, and for making decisions that will benefit your future.

Interpretation and Mantra...

You are handling several tasks at once and must exercise time management to establish equilibrium. You don't necessarily need to be occupied to accomplish your goals. On occasion, taking a break can be the most productive decision you make.

Mantra "I balance my responsibilities, adapt to change, and find stability in the midst of chaos."

The card the guides have chosen for you is...

The Tarot The Sun represents positivity, happiness, and joy. It is a symbol of growth, renewal, and hope, and often signifies a time of great accomplishment and success. In a reading, The Sun suggests that the individual is on the right path and that good things are ahead. It encourages them to embrace their positive qualities and let their light shine. This can indicate that happiness, success, and prosperity are within reach and that the individual has the power to manifest their desires. It also suggests a time of self-discovery and inner growth, and encourages the individual to trust in their own abilities and trust the journey. Overall, The Sun is a sign of optimism and encourages the individual to embrace their positive qualities and celebrate their successes.

Interpretation and Mantra...

You are encompassed by warmth, brightness, and vigor. You are illuminated and revitalized by opportunities, progress, and triumph. Emit your radiance and illuminate the world around you.

Mantra *"I radiate positivity and joy, and trust in my own inner light."*

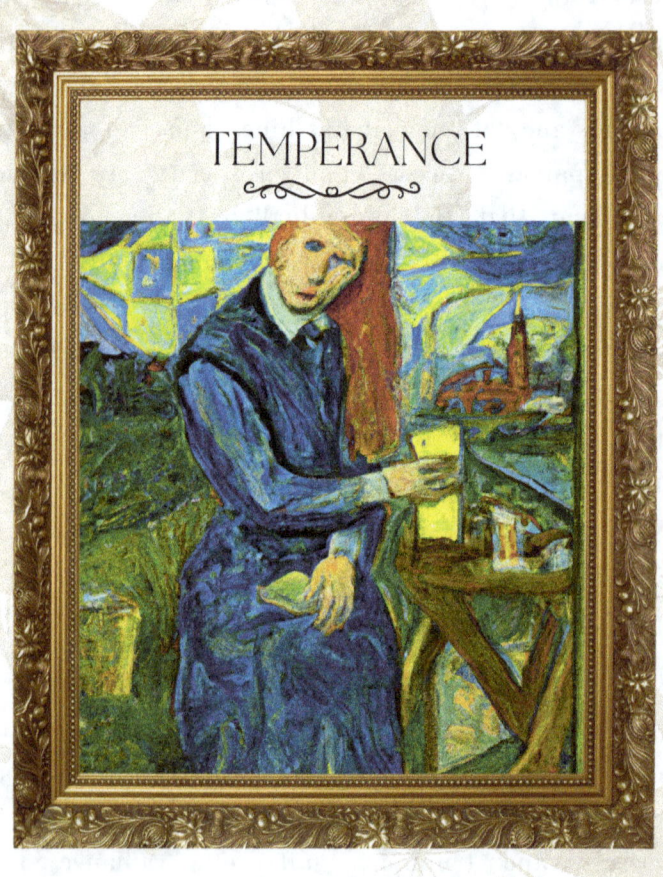

The card the guides have chosen for you is...

Temperance represents balance, harmony, and moderation. It is often associated with the astrological sign of Sagittarius and is traditionally depicted as an angel or angelic figure holding a chalice and pouring liquid between two cups. It is often interpreted as a reminder to find balance in one's life and to approach situations with patience and self-control. In a reading, Temperance can indicate a need to reconcile opposing forces or to find a middle ground in a situation. It may also suggest that a period of reflection and introspection is needed to bring about a sense of balance and stability. In a more negative context, the Temperance can indicate a lack of balance or self-control and a need to take a step back and evaluate one's actions. Overall, Temperance is a positive and uplifting symbol of balance, harmony, and self-control.

Interpretation and Mantra...

You are uncovering the means to establish equilibrium and concordance in your existence. You experience synchronization and tranquility with your external environment.

Mantra: "I create Order out of Chaos."

THE DEVIL

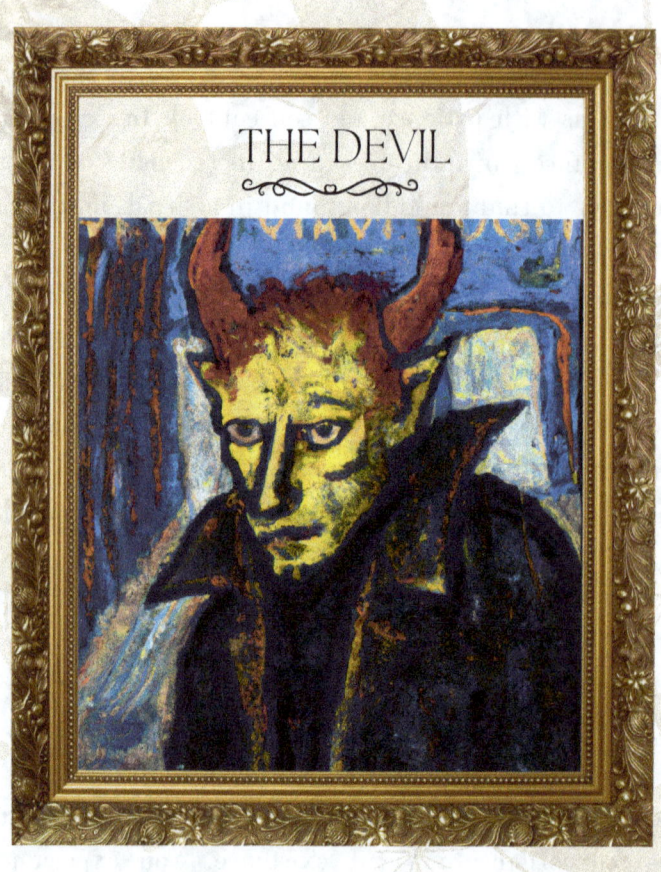

The card the guides have chosen for you is...

The Devil tarot is typically associated with materialism, addiction, and being enslaved to one's desires. It represents being controlled by one's base impulses, such as greed and lust, and being in a state of spiritual bondage. The image often depicts a horned figure, similar to the Devil in traditional Christian imagery, holding a torch and standing on a pedestal of stone blocks. This imagery is meant to suggest that the person being represented by the Devil is being held back by their own vices and is unable to break free. However, the Devil can also suggest that the person is aware of their own weaknesses and is actively working to overcome them. Ultimately, the Devil serves as a reminder that we all have our own personal demons to battle, but that with self-awareness and determination, we can (and will) overcome them..

Interpretation and Mantra...

You recognize that detrimental attachments, addictions, and dependencies are impacting you. Although it may seem challenging to release them, it is simpler than you perceive. Release your fear and let go.

Mantra "I break free from my bonds and rise above my desires."

FOUR OF SWORDS

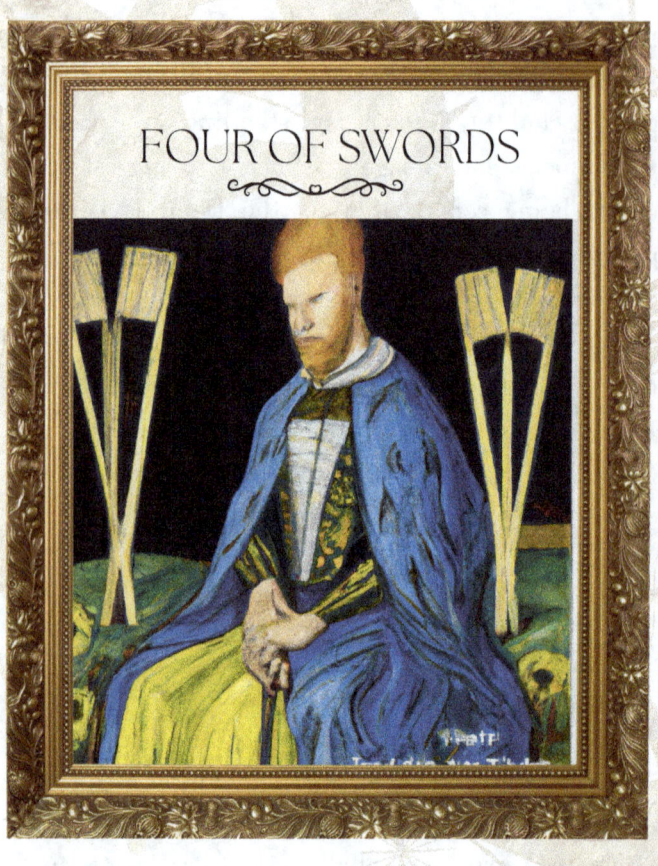

The card the guides have chosen for you is...

The Four of Swords tarot represents rest, recovery, and contemplation. The Four of Swords can indicate that the querent is in a time of rest and recovery, and that they are being called to take a break from their daily activities and to reflect on their current situation. It suggests a feeling of being mentally and physically exhausted, and the need for some time alone to recharge. The Four of Swords also represents the ability to find inner peace and to make sense of the past. It can indicate that the querent will have to take time for themselves to reflect and make sense of recent events, in order to move forward. In a negative context, it may indicate that the querent is avoiding their problems and responsibilities. Overall, the Four of Swords is a reminder to take time for yourself, to rest and reflect, and to find inner peace in order to move forward.

Interpretation and Mantra...

You have achieved a significant accomplishment, and it's time to replenish your energy before moving onto the next phase. Allow yourself to rest, clear your mind, and engage in meditation.

Mantra "I take time to rest, reflect and find inner peace, allowing my mind and body to recover and recharge."

FIVE OF WANDS

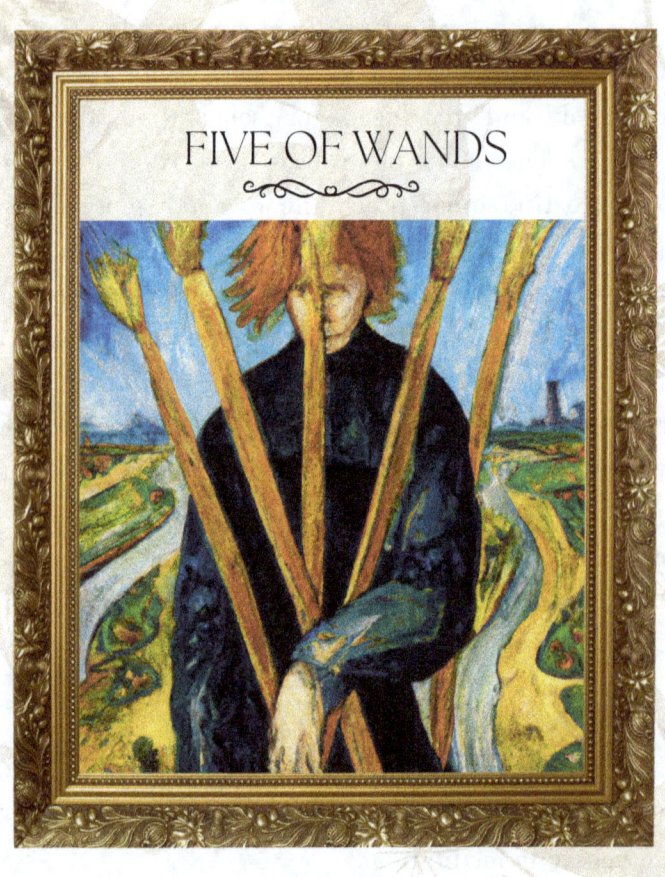

The card the guides have chosen for you is...

The Five of Wands in the tarot deck represents competition, conflict and struggles. It suggests that you are facing challenges and obstacles in your life and are possibly grappling with various conflicting interests. The image on the card usually shows five people fighting with wands, symbolizing the internal battles you may be experiencing. It may also indicate external rivalries, where you are competing against others for a shared goal. However, the Five of Wands is also a reminder that challenges are opportunities for growth and that you can rise above any difficulties by being resilient and resourceful. Embrace the competition, stay focused on your goals and don't let others bring you down.

Interpretation and Mantra...

There is a lot of turmoil, dissension, rivalry, and internal conflict around you. Everyone is expressing their viewpoints, but there is a lack of attentive listening. Either make a deliberate effort to attentively listen to each person or consider removing yourself from the tense situation.

Mantra "I embrace competition and overcome challenges with grace and determination."

SEVEN OF WANDS

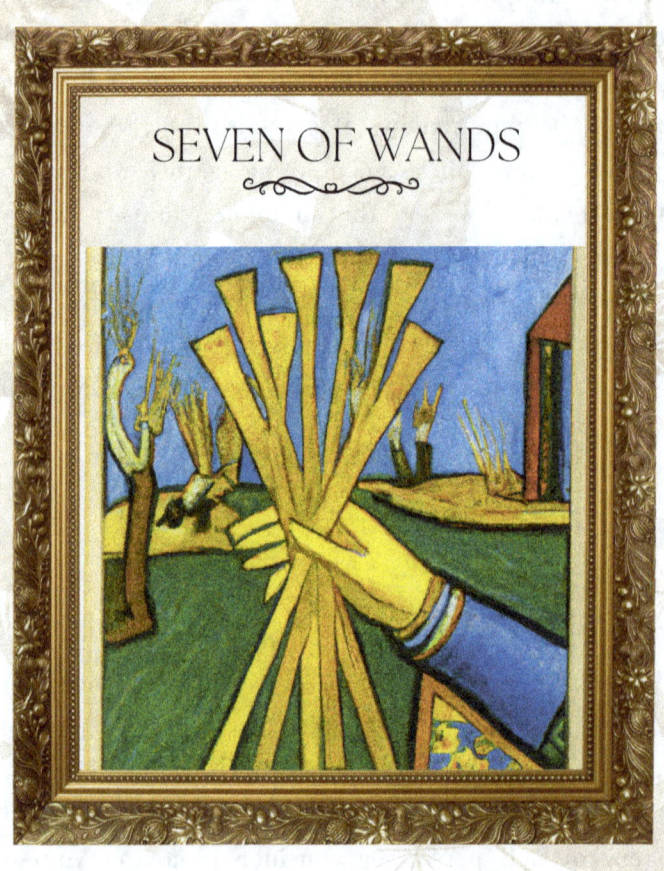

The card the guides have chosen for you is...

The Seven of Wands tarot represents a time of challenge and competition. It symbolizes standing up for oneself, fighting for what one believes in, and being defensive. It suggests that there may be obstacles in the way, but it is necessary to be strong, determined, and confident in order to overcome them. The Seven of Wands also signifies the need to be resourceful and to find innovative solutions in order to succeed. This card can represent a competitive environment, such as in the workplace, where it is important to assert oneself in order to succeed. Overall, the Seven of Wands suggests that it is time to stand tall, fight for what is important, and believe in oneself.

Interpretation and Mantra...

You're in a desirable situation. You've put in a lot of effort to reach where you are, however, there are others who covet your accomplishments and may be willing to compete with you. It's important to safeguard your position and assert your convictions.

Mantra "*I am strong, I am resilient, I will overcome the challenges that come my way.*"

The card the guides have chosen for you is...

The Tarot Strength represents inner strength, courage, and determination. It is associated with the fire element, which represents energy, passion, and drive. Strength symbolizes a time of inner fortitude, courage, and the ability to overcome challenges and obstacles. It may indicate that you are facing challenges or obstacles, but that you have the inner strength, courage, and determination to overcome them. Strength can also suggest that you are able to harness your passions, energy, and drive to achieve your goals and overcome obstacles. It is a reminder to tap into your inner strength and courage, to be determined and persistent in pursuing your goals, and to remain calm and focused even in the face of challenges or difficulties. Strength suggests that it's a time for harnessing your inner fortitude, courage, and determination to achieve your goals and overcome any obstacles that may arise.

Interpretation and Mantra...

You possess an inner power and resilience, and exercise leadership through delicate influence and persuasion. You are aware of your primal instincts and exhibit both your raw strength and bravery along with calculated restraint.

Mantra "*I am strong, courageous, and determined. I face challenges with grace and inner fortitude.*"

THE LOVERS

The card the guides have chosen for you is...

The Lovers tarot represents love, relationships, and deep emotional connections. It symbolizes the choice between temptation and commitment, and often indicates a significant personal or romantic relationship. The Lovers usually features two figures gazing into each other's eyes, reflecting the strong emotional connection and mutual love between them. The Lovers can also represent a need for self-discovery and the importance of making choices based on your values and inner voice. This may also indicate a major decision or turning point in a relationship, and can suggest the need to trust your instincts and follow your heart. Overall, the Lovers tarot is a powerful symbol of love, passion, and commitment, reminding us to cherish the relationships that bring meaning and fulfillment to our lives.

Interpretation and Mantra...

You have a deep, meaningful connection with someone that honors both of your souls. You are able to integrate two opposing forces into a unified state, and now face a decision that requires the utmost integrity and morality.

Mantra "I trust in the power of love and choose to follow my heart. I cultivate deep and meaningful relationships with those who bring joy and fulfillment to my life."

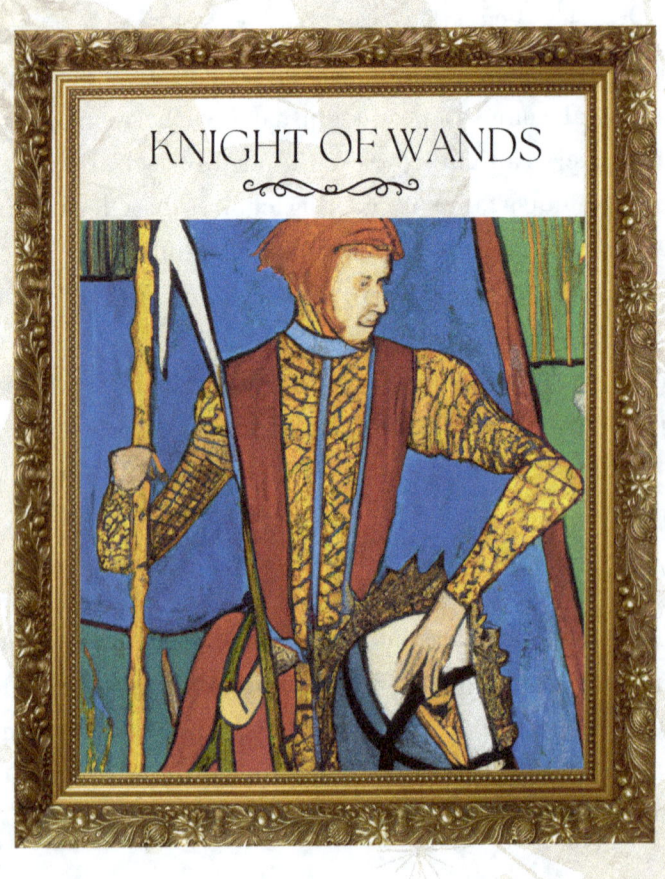

The card the guides have chosen for you is...

The Knight of Wands in a tarot reading represents movement, action, and passion. It suggests that the querent is about to embark on a new journey or venture, filled with excitement and enthusiasm. This card can indicate that the querent is feeling restless and needs to take action to pursue their goals and passions. The Knight of Wands also represents a free spirit and a love of adventure, indicating that the querent may be feeling a desire for new experiences and challenges. In a negative context, it may indicate impulsiveness and a lack of planning. Overall, the Knight of Wands is a call to action and a reminder to follow your passions and take risks.

Interpretation and Mantra...

You are brimming with energy, zeal, drive, and eagerness, channeling this force through your inspired actions. Driven by your self-assurance and ambitiousness, you are determined to effect change and accomplish your goals.

Mantra "I take action with passion and purpose, following my dreams and pursuing my goals with determination and enthusiasm."

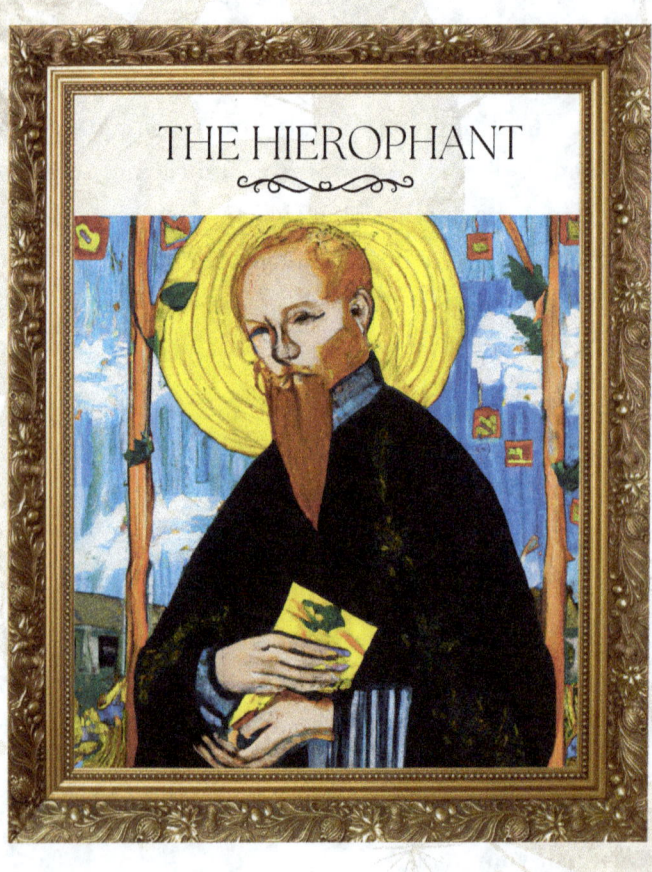

The card the guides have chosen for you is...

The Hierophant, also known as the Pope or the High Priest, it is a major arcana tarot. It typically represents religious or spiritual guidance, tradition, and conformity to established beliefs. The Hierophant is often associated with teachers, priests, or other spiritual leaders who help to guide individuals on their spiritual journey. In a reading, the Hierophant can indicate the need for guidance or a teacher to help navigate difficult times or to provide a new perspective. It can also suggest that it is time to conform to a specific set of beliefs or traditions, or to seek out a deeper understanding of one's faith or spirituality. Additionally, it can also indicate the need for a break from a traditional approach and to seek the unconventional.

Interpretation and Mantra...

As you collaborate with a teacher, mentor, or trusted authority, you will enhance your knowledge and gain a deeper understanding of fundamental principles.

Mantra "I trust in my spiritual guide and align with my inner wisdom"

The card the guides have chosen for you is...

The Fool in the Tarot deck is often depicted as a carefree and joyful traveler, starting a new journey with a sense of wonder and excitement. The Fool represents new beginnings, potential, and trust in the unknown. In a reading, this symbolizes the need to take a leap of faith and step out of your comfort zone. It encourages you to embrace change and see the world through fresh eyes. The Fool can also represent a sense of innocence, impulsiveness, and a lack of caution, reminding you to be mindful of your actions and decisions. The Fool asks you to trust in yourself and the universe, as you step out into the unknown and embark on a new journey filled with endless possibilities..

Interpretation and Mantra...

You have a chance to explore new horizons and embark on fresh endeavors. Maintain an open mind and a curious attitude, willing to discover and learn novel concepts. Engage in playful activities, enjoy yourself, and be spontaneous.

Mantra "*I trust my intuition and embrace new adventures with courage and positivity.*"

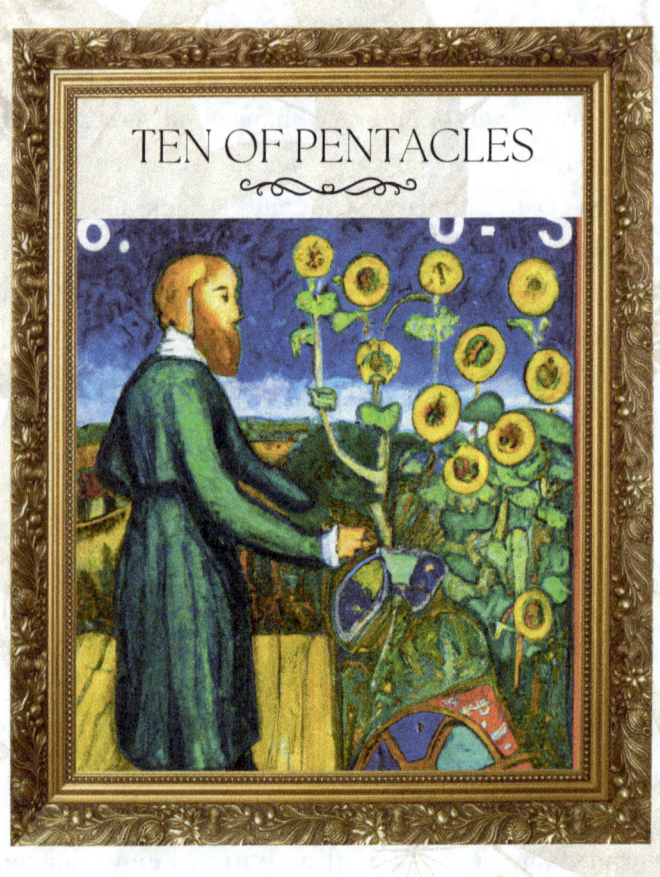

The card the guides have chosen for you is...

The Ten of Pentacles tarot represents wealth, prosperity, and financial stability. It symbolizes a sense of security and a sense of accomplishment, often reflecting a time of abundance and stability in one's financial and personal life. The image often depicts a family gathered together, symbolizing the importance of family and community in building and maintaining wealth. The Ten of Pentacles also represents a sense of completion and fulfillment, often indicating that one has achieved their goals and is now reaping the rewards of their hard work. This can suggest that one is ready to pass down their wealth and knowledge to future generations. However, it can also indicate a need for caution, as too much focus on material wealth can lead to neglect of other important aspects of life. The Ten of Pentacles tarot is a powerful symbol of wealth, prosperity, and a strong sense of community.

Interpretation and Mantra...

You have diligently worked and devoted yourself to accumulate wealth and abundance. It fills you with great joy and satisfaction to share your wealth with those you love. You express gratitude for achieving your material goals and fulfilling your dreams.

Mantra *"I attract abundance and prosperity in all areas of my life. I value my family and community, and work to build wealth and stability for myself and those I love."*

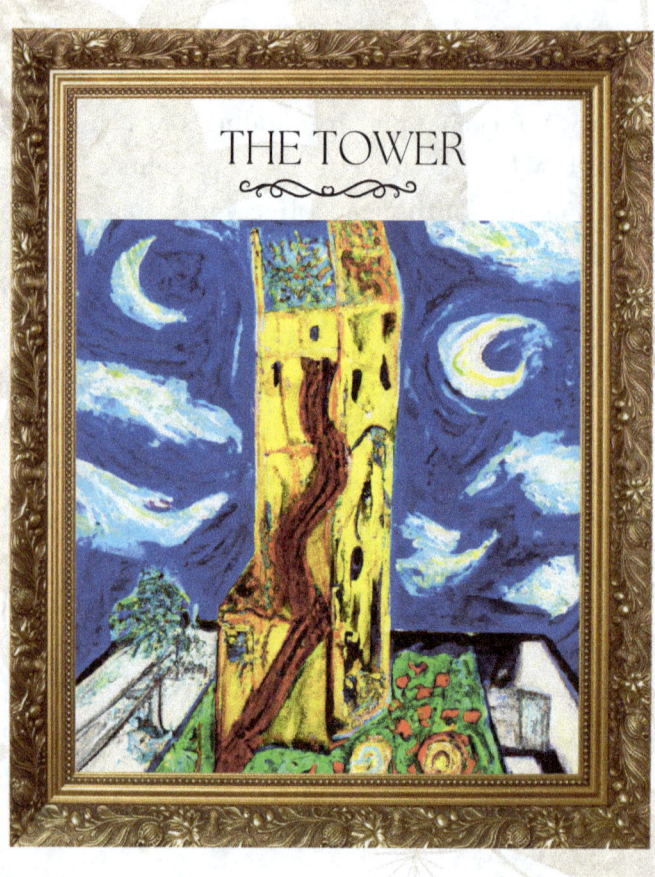

The card the guides have chosen for you is...

The Tarot The Tower often represents sudden upheaval, chaos, and unexpected change. It can indicate a sense of instability and a loss of control, as well as warning of potential danger or conflict. However, it can also symbolize a necessary break from old patterns and ways of thinking, leading to growth and transformation. In a reading, The Tower asks the individual to face their fears and be prepared for change, as it may bring about a new perspective and understanding. This suggests that what may initially seem like a negative event can ultimately lead to positive growth and liberation. Trusting the process and embracing change can help navigate the challenges the tower represents

Interpretation and Mantra...

The very foundations that you believed to be stable are collapsing around you, causing chaos and destruction. However, it's important to recognize that these events are occurring for your benefit, not as a punishment. Novel paradigms and prospects are appearing, and eventually, you will comprehend their purpose.

Mantra "I am ready to face the storm and embrace change."

Journal Pages.

The Angels are always with you.

My daily thoughts....

My daily thoughts....

My daily thoughts....

My daily thoughts....

My daily thoughts....

My daily thoughts....

My daily thoughts....

My daily thoughts....

My daily thoughts....

My daily thoughts....

My daily thoughts....

Disclaimer: The Daily Angel Tarot book provides information on tarot readings and interpretation, but it is not intended as a substitute for professional advice, diagnosis, or treatment. The information contained in this book is provided for educational and entertainment purposes only and is not meant to be taken as specific advice for individual circumstances. The author and publisher make no representations or warranties with respect to the accuracy or completeness of the contents of this book and specifically disclaim any implied warranties of merchantability or fitness for a particular purpose. The reader should always consult with a licensed professional for any specific concerns or questions. The author and publisher shall not be liable for any loss or damage caused or alleged to have been caused, directly or indirectly, by the information contained in this book. The use of this book is at the reader's sole risk

www.ingramcontent.com/pod-product-compliance
Lightning Source LLC
Chambersburg PA
CBHW051432290426
44109CB00016B/1520